orship
ideas
for Youth
Ministry
Volume 2

Group
Loveland, Colorado

Worship Ideas for Youth Ministry, Volume 2

Credits

Editor: Amy Simpson
Chief Creative Officer: Joani Schultz
Copy Editor: Alison Imbriaco
Art Director: Randy Kady
Cover Art Director: Jeff A. Storm
Designer: Randy Kady
Cover Designer: Diana Walters
Computer Graphic Artist: Joyce Douglas
Illustrator: Randy Kady
Production Manager: Peggy Naylor

Library of Congress Cataloging-in-Publication Data
      (Revised for Volume 2)
    Worship ideas for youth ministry.
      p. cm.
    Includes indexes.
  1. Worship programs. 2. Church group work with youth.
  3. Bible. N.T. Gospels-Liturgical use. I. Group Publishing.
  BV29.W64 1997
  264—dc21
ISBN 0-7644-2002-X (v. 1)
ISBN 0-7644-2079-8 (v. 2)   97-7449
                                                CIP

10 9 8 7 6 5 4 3 2 1   08 07 06 05 04 03 02 01 00 99

Printed in the United States of America.

Contents

• worship ideas for youth ministry, volume 2 •

index

Contributors

We'd like to thank the following people, who contributed their creative
ideas and hard work to this collection.
Tim Baker
Karen Dockrey
Debbie Gowensmith
Michele Howe
Mikal Keefer
Jan Kershner
Dennis R. McLaughlin
Julie Meiklejohn
Pamela J. Shoup
Trevor Simpson

Introduction

Introduction

"They held harps given them by God and sang the song of Moses the servant of God and the song of the Lamb:
'Great and marvelous are your deeds,
    Lord God Almighty.
Just and true are your ways,
    King of the ages.
Who will not fear you, O Lord,
    and bring glory to your name?
For you alone are holy.
All nations will come
    and worship before you,
for your righteous acts have been revealed.' "
(Revelation 15:2b-4)

Worship is standing in awe of who God is, what God has done, and what God continues to do. Our God is eternal, all-knowing, all-powerful, completely holy, and full of perfect love. All God's acts are blameless. Although we can't fully know or understand God's character, we must respond in awe when we are faced with God's presence.

"When the parents brought in the child Jesus to do for him what the custom of the Law required, Simeon took him in his arms and praised God, saying:
'Sovereign Lord, as you have promised,
    you now dismiss your servant in peace.
For my eyes have seen your salvation,
    which you have prepared in the sight of all people,
a light for revelation to the Gentiles
    and for glory to your people Israel.' "
(Luke 2:27b-32)

Worship is a natural response to God's love and grace. When we truly realize what God has done for us, we can't help but be overwhelmed by God's marvelous character. Almighty God, the creator of the universe, the perfect and holy one, descended from heaven in deliberate vulnerability. Jesus took on our sin and died in our place, giving us the chance to stand before God as if we had never sinned. He gave the ultimate sacrifice on our behalf so we can have a relationship with God.

Introduction

"**G**od has ascended amid shouts of joy,
the Lord amid the sounding of trumpets.
Sing praises to God, sing praises;
sing praises to our King, sing praises.
For God is the King of all the earth;
sing to him a psalm of praise.
God reigns over the nations;
God is seated on his holy throne.
The nobles of the nations assemble
as the people of the God of Abraham,
for the kings of the earth belong to God;
he is greatly exalted."
(Psalm 47:5-9)

Worship is acknowledging our place in the universe in relationship to God. True worship comes from a heart that knows the power and perspective of God as greater than our own. Expressing God's greatness can deepen our understanding of the fact that even though we don't comprehend God's work and we can't see God's plan, we can trust that God is in control.

Worship Ideas for Youth Ministry, Volume 2 is a collection of creative, unique, varied, and inspiring worship experiences for any youth group. These worship ideas include traditional forms of worship as well as exciting, new ideas. And every idea will draw your students toward meaningful communion with God.

Each worship idea in this book is based on a specific Scripture passage in the New Testament. Use a worship idea at the beginning of a youth meeting on a specific Scripture passage, during a meeting on a biblical theme, or by itself, in place of a regular youth meeting. You may also want to allow your students to lead the entire congregation in worship. Refer to the indexes in the back of the book (pp. 121-124) to find the worship ideas you need.

Use this book to get your youth excited about worship. The variety of fresh ideas will help them think and talk about what it means to worship and will lead them to life-changing encounters with the love, majesty, and person of God.

Acts

Scripture: Acts 2:1-21

Theme: The Holy Spirit

Experience: In this **creative reading**, teenagers will celebrate the early Christians' experience of receiving the Holy Spirit at Pentecost. This activity is most effective in a camp setting, at night around a campfire.

Preparation: You'll need four photocopies of the "Everyone Who Calls On the Name of the Lord" handout (p. 8) and four flashlights.

Before the experience, choose four teenagers who are good readers, and assign them the parts of the readers in the creative reading. Consider giving readers photocopies of the handout ahead of time so they can familiarize themselves with it.

Just before the experience, have the four readers position themselves separately in the shadows beyond reach of the campfire light. For example, the readers might go to the four corners just beyond the immediate area. Give each reader a flashlight to use in reading the script.

Worship

You may want to introduce the reading by asking teenagers to share what they know about the coming of the Holy Spirit at Pentecost, or you may choose to summarize the events briefly (see Acts 1 for the events leading up to Pentecost).

After your introduction, ask teenagers to sit quietly and listen as they think about what that Pentecost experience might have been like. Direct your readers to begin the creative reading.

When the reading is over, you may want to ask these questions:

● **What do you think it would have been like to be present at Pentecost when God sent the Holy Spirit?**

● **What is the importance of the Holy Spirit coming into the lives of Christians?**

● **Describe an experience you've had involving the Holy Spirit.**

Scripture: Acts 2:36-47

Theme: Sacrifice

Experience: In this **act of commitment**, teenagers will commit to sacrificing for others.

Preparation: You'll need Bibles, newsprint, markers, chairs, and index cards.

Handout

Everyone Who Calls On the Name of the Lord

(based on Acts 2:1-21)

Reader 1: It was really strange!

Reader 2: Jesus had been taken into the clouds before their very eyes.

Reader 3: Taken up to sit at the right hand of God.

Reader 4: "When the day of Pentecost came, they were all together in one place."

Reader 1: "Suddenly a sound like the blowing of a violent wind came from heaven and filled the whole house where they were sitting."

Reader 2: Yes, it was like a violent wind.

Reader 3: They had never experienced anything like it.

Reader 4: It was the strangest thing they'd ever experienced.

Reader 1: Then something happened that was even stranger!

Reader 4: Stranger?

Reader 3: What could be stranger than a sound like a violent wind filling the house?

Reader 2: "They saw what seemed to be tongues of fire that separated and came to rest on each of them."

Reader 4: And they weren't burned?

Reader 1: No! They were filled with the Holy Spirit.

Reader 3: The Holy Spirit?

Reader 2: Yes! And they began to speak in other languages as the Spirit enabled them.

Reader 4: That sounds really strange!

Reader 1: Very strange! There were people from all nations who gathered around in bewilderment.

Reader 2: They were amazed, and they wanted to know why they were speaking in different languages.

Reader 1: They were amazed and perplexed, and asked one another, "What does this mean?"

Reader 3: It sounds to me as if they'd had too much wine.

Reader 2: That's exactly what those who were watching thought too!

Reader 1: But Peter stood up.

Reader 4: He raised his voice!

Reader 2: He addressed the crowd!

Reader 3: *(skeptically)* I can't wait to hear what he said.

Reader 4: What he said?

Reader 1: He said, "These men are not drunk, as you suppose."

Reader 2: "In the last days, God says, I will pour out my Spirit on all people."

Reader 3: "Your sons and daughters will prophesy..."

Reader 4: "Your young men will see visions..."

Reader 1: "Your old men will dream dreams."

Reader 2: "I will show wonders in the heaven above and signs on the earth below."

Reader 4: "And everyone who calls on the name of the Lord will be saved."

Reader 2: "And everyone who calls on the name of the Lord will be saved.'

Reader 1: "And everyone who calls on the name of the Lord will be saved."

Reader 3: "And everyone who calls on the name of the Lord will be saved."

Acts

Worship

Have teenagers form groups of four and read Acts 2:36-41. When groups have read the passage, ask:

● What did you notice about God's power in this passage?
● What does it mean to "Repent and be baptized"?
● How did people who believed in Christ live at this time?

Say: **In the very beginning of the church, people were becoming Christians in large numbers. And as people were getting to know Christ, they were also getting to know a new lifestyle.**

Have groups read Acts 2:42-47. Ask:

● What type of lifestyle did the early believers live?
● Is it possible for us to live the same type of lifestyle? Explain.
● Would you want to live this way? Why or why not?

Say: **Knowing Jesus is an incredible experience, and sometimes knowing Jesus causes our lifestyles to change. God's Word tells us it was common for Christians to make sacrifices for other people. As Christians, we should be willing to sell our belongings or give them away to help meet the needs of other people. It's important to remember, though, that this type of lifestyle is the result of belief in Jesus, not a way to earn God's favor. Let's brainstorm things we could sacrifice for others.**

Give each group a marker and a sheet of newsprint. Have each group make a list of items they'd be willing to sacrifice for others. Encourage teenagers to think of as many items as they can. Be sure to participate with at least one group, naming items you would be willing to sacrifice for others. When they've made their lists, have groups present them and post them on the wall. When all the lists are posted, say:

You've done a great job identifying some things you could sacrifice for others. Now let's start sacrificing.

Arrange chairs in a semicircle to make an altar. Ask teenagers to sit quietly on the floor facing the altar and think about the sacrifices they're willing to commit to. When they've had time to think, distribute markers and index cards.

Have teenagers write or draw on their cards descriptions of specific items they'll sacrifice for others. (Don't forget to write or draw on your own card.) When they've finished the descriptions, have teenagers quietly place their cards on the altar.

When all the cards have been placed on the altar, lead the group in a prayer of dedication. Ask God to help you and your students keep the commitments you've made. As you dismiss the teenagers, encourage them to remember their commitments and to follow through by sacrificing for others.

Acts

Scripture: Acts 3:11-19

Theme: Forgiveness

Experience: In this **prayer of confession,** teenagers will write apology notes to God for sins they've committed, then discuss how faith in Jesus can make them whole.

Preparation: You'll need colored construction paper, scissors, newsprint, tape, markers, and Bibles.

Before the experience, cut the sheets of colored construction paper in half horizontally. You'll need one half-sheet for each student. Tape a sheet of newsprint to a wall in your meeting area, and draw the outline of a large cross on the newsprint.

Worship

Give each person a half-sheet of construction paper and a marker. Have each teenager fold the paper in half to resemble a card.

Say: **We're going to write notes of apology to God. Think of something you've done wrong recently that might have disappointed God. Then think of one word that represents that sin, and write that word on the inside of the card.**

For example, if your sin was yelling at your sister, you could write "anger" or "words." You won't have to describe your sin or tell anyone else about it—you'll just tell God.

Give teenagers a few moments to write, then say:

In the book of Acts, Peter talked about sin. Let's look at the passage.

Distribute Bibles, and have teenagers form pairs to read Acts 3:11-19 together. When the teenagers have finished reading, have pairs discuss the following questions. After each question, let pairs share their insights with the rest of the group. Ask:

● **How does the sin you wrote down compare to the sins Peter was describing?**

● **Do you think your sins are any less "sinful" than the ones described in this passage? Explain.**

Say: **The Bible says Jesus died on the cross for our sins. That means not only that Jesus died to pay for the sins of the people who crucified him, but also that he died for the sins we commit today—the very sin you wrote on your paper.** Ask:

● **What does it mean to repent?**

● **How can you repent of the sin you wrote down?**

Say: **In this passage, Peter said the crippled man was healed because of his faith in Jesus. It's through faith in Jesus that we receive**

Acts

forgiveness for our sins. Jesus already paid the price for the sin you wrote down. I'd like each of you to say a silent prayer, confessing and asking for forgiveness for the sin you wrote on your paper.

Give teenagers a few moments to pray. Then say:

Think of one word that describes how you feel knowing that Jesus' death made your forgiveness possible. Write that one word on the outside of your card, then come forward and tape your card to the inside of this cross.

After teenagers tape their cards to the cross, say:

Look at the papers on our cross—our sins are covered with words of joy and thanksgiving. That's what God wants for us. God knows that, just like the crippled man in Acts, we need repentance and faith to be made whole. And it's the Cross that makes that possible. We're the ones who benefit from repentance. God doesn't *need* our apologies to forgive us. If he hadn't wanted to forgive us, he wouldn't have watched his Son suffer on the cross. God wants our apologies because he knows that only through our repentance and faith can we be made whole.

Close with a prayer similar to this:

Dear Lord, thank you for taking our sins to the cross with you. And thank you for making us whole when we repent and believe. Amen.

Scripture: Acts 4:1-13

Theme: God's power

Experience: In this dramatic presentation and sharing time, teenagers will tell each other about the transforming work of God in their lives.

Preparation: You'll need a Bible, paper, colorful markers, and a hand mirror for every two or three people in your group.

Worship

Have teenagers sit in a circle. Read Acts 4:1-13 aloud to the group. Point out that Peter and John shared the good news of Jesus' resurrection with the people, even thought they knew the Sadducees would be angered. At the trial, the disciples continued to boldly proclaim their faith in the saving work of Christ.

Say: **Peter and John were probably afraid. They knew who they were up against. Even more important, Peter and John must have compared themselves to their enemies, who were the richest, best dressed, most influential men of their time. Still, the disciples knew God's power was at work in them.**

Give each person a piece of paper and a marker. Have teenagers form groups of three or four. Instruct each group to plan a commercial that demonstrates God's power in the lives of people by comparing old and new "versions" of themselves—before and after God's power entered their lives.

For example, one commercial might show two people walking down the street when a car drives by and splashes them with mud. Reacting with anger, they yell at the car's driver and pick up stones to throw at the car.

The next scene might begin exactly the same way as the same two people are splashed by the same driver. This time, however, the people look at each other, shrug their shoulders, and calmly alter their plans so that they can run home and change clothes. One character looks at the other and remarks how amazing it is that they didn't react with anger. As in any good commercial, the second character would point out that the change has come from God's power. That character might look at the audience and say, "God's power to change...Get it...today!"

When each group has planned a commercial, have groups perform their commercials for each other. Then reread Acts 4:13. Say:

● **What did the people notice most about Peter and John?**

● **How was the church affected by God's power to transform un-educated men into well-spoken, bold witnesses?**

● **How can we affect our world today when we rely on God's power to change us?**

Say: **Peter and John weren't educated men, yet they stood with courage before the most educated men of their day. The Holy Spirit rested on them, telling them what to say. And God will do the same for us today.**

Have teenagers form groups of two or three, encouraging them to form groups with people they know well. Give a mirror to each group.

Leader Tip

Say: **In your group, take turns looking at yourself in the mirror and telling your partner or partners what you see. Instead of describing your physical appearance, though, describe your character strengths or weaknesses or your personality traits. For example, you may say you see an outgoing personality, intelligence, and a good sense of humor.**

Partners, as your friend is sharing, listen and stop that person each time you hear him or her say something negative. Then have the person repeat the statement from God's viewpoint or by relying on God's transforming power. For example, if someone says she's disor-

If you have newcomers or visitors in the group, pair them with adults or mature teenagers. If necessary, encourage partners in these pairs to spend a few moments talking and getting to know each other before they do the exercise.

ganized, stop her and encourage her to reword the statement. This time she might point out that she's spontaneous and flexible.

Encourage students to take turns holding the mirror and sharing. When everyone has had a chance to share, have the teenagers take turns praying for their partners to be courageous in sharing their faith.

Scripture: Acts 5:17-32

Theme: Sharing faith

Experience: In this **service opportunity**, teenagers will present a Bible lesson to a class of children.

Preparation: You'll need Bibles.

Before the experience, arrange for your group of teenagers to teach a lesson to an elementary school class.

Worship

Read Acts 5:17-32 aloud. Have teenagers form groups of four or five, and ask groups to discuss these questions:

● What is the most amazing part of this passage to you? Why?

● What have you been so passionate about in your life that you would stand up for it as the apostles did, even if it meant being threatened?

● Would you have done what the apostles did, or would you have chosen another course of action? Explain.

● What would you do if you were told that you could be arrested if you told others about Jesus?

After ten to fifteen minutes of discussion, call for the group's attention and say:

Fortunately, we're free to share the good news of God's Word with other people. That's exactly what we're going to do now. We're going to prepare a lesson based on the Scripture reading and teach it to an elementary class.

Have teenagers form two teams. Assign Team 1 the responsibility of creating a short skit based on Acts 5:17-32.

Assign Team 2 the responsibility of leading a short discussion with the elementary class. Team 2 should prepare two or three open-ended questions to help the children understand the passage. (An open-ended question is one that can't be answered "yes" or "no.") If the elementary class is large, have the teenagers consider asking the children to form small groups for discussion. The teenagers can be discussion leaders for the groups.

After approximately twenty minutes of preparation, bring the two teams back together. Have them run through the lesson together.

After the practice run, assist teenagers in presenting their lesson to the elementary class. After they've taught the class, bring them back together for a short discussion. Ask:

● What did you learn from the experience?

● Did anything happen that you didn't expect? If so, what?

● In what ways do you think God used you to spread his Word?

● How was this experience like what happened to the apostles in the Scripture passage we read?

● In what ways was it different?

● What are some other ways we can teach others about God's Word?

Scripture: Acts 7:51-60

Theme: Obedience

Experience: In this **prayer of confession,** teenagers will take time to contemplate their own obedience to God and commit to obey.

Preparation: You'll need a Bible; paper; pens or pencils; permanent markers; and one small, flat stone for each person.

Worship

Read Acts 7:51-60 aloud.

Say: **Stephen called the people "stiff-necked," which means "stub-born" or "obstinate," and he accused them of resisting the work of the Holy Spirit. In what ways could God say the same about us today? Listen to the following areas where we might struggle to obey God:**

● **obedience in honoring our parents' wishes even when we disagree;**

● **obedience in fulfilling the requests of teachers, employers, and church leaders;**

● **obedience in respecting our friends' desires and needs; and**

● **obedience to the Holy Spirit's prompting to not participate in things we know would not honor Christ.**

Give each person paper and a pen or pencil. Reread the four areas of obedience described above. Ask teenagers to write down one specific example for each of the four areas that describes a time they've disobeyed.

Say: **For example, maybe your parents left for the day and told you no parties were allowed, but three friends showed up and wanted to invite more, so you did. Maybe you left work a half hour early when your boss was gone and you'd finished all your work. Maybe a troubled friend confided in you, and then you slipped and told someone else.**

After each person has completed a list, say:

Disobeying can be quite subtle. We may not even realize we're

doing it. Although Stephen's accusers disobeyed God openly and in front of everyone, our sins of disobedience are no less serious or wrong if they're hidden. God wants us to learn to obey quickly and ask for forgiveness quickly. Let's take some time to confess our disobedience to God.

Pray aloud, asking the Holy Spirit to search each heart to reveal any hidden disobedience. Then allow a few moments of silent prayer. After a few moments, suggest to students that they tear their papers as a symbolic gesture of turning away from disobedience.

Give each person a small, flat stone and a permanent marker. Instruct teenagers to write the words "quick to obey" on one side of the rocks. Then have the teenagers turn the rocks over and write a word or symbol that represents a struggle with disobedience. Tell teenagers to take their stones home with them as reminders to obey.

Scripture: Acts 8:26-40

Theme: Spiritual growth

Experience: In this **artistic experience** and **sharing time**, teenagers will praise God for people and events that have influenced their spiritual growth.

Preparation: You'll need Bibles, a piece of newsprint for each person, and colorful markers.

Worship

Have teenagers form pairs. Ask one member of each pair to read Acts 8:26-40 to his or her partner. Then have the partner summarize the passage. Have the pairs discuss the following questions:

● If this story were written about you, would you have been more like the Ethiopian man, Philip, or an uninvolved bystander? Explain why.

● Philip followed the directions of the Lord. When have you done something you believe God wanted you to do?

● When have you failed to do what you thought God wanted you to do?

● How would this story have been different if Philip hadn't followed God's direction?

● What people and events in your life have most influenced your spiritual growth?

After allowing time for discussion, give each person a piece of newsprint, and set out colorful markers where everyone can use them.

Say: **Think about all those people and events that have influenced your spiritual growth. Then draw a map of them. You can make a map that shows your spiritual journey year-by-year, by different locations, or by the events themselves. The key is to be creative and** include as many people and events as you can think of.

Allow fifteen to twenty minutes for teenagers to create their maps. When everyone has finished, have teenagers explain their maps to the rest of the group, praising God for the people and events in their lives.

Scripture: Acts 9:1-20

Theme: Spreading God's Word

Experience: In this **commissioning** and **dramatic presentation**, teenagers will identify how they have persecuted Christ in their lives and ask the Holy Spirit to help them spread God's Word.

Preparation: You'll need a photocopy of "Saul's Conversion" script (p. 18) for each person.

Before the experience, designate a stage area and set a chair on one side of it.

Worship

Give each person a copy of "Saul's Conversion" script. Assign the parts of Saul, Jesus, a Soldier, and Ananias. The rest of the group can be soldiers traveling with Saul or disciples with Saul in Damascus.

After you've finished the skit, have teenagers form groups of three or four and discuss these questions:

● **By persecuting Christians or the church, how did Saul persecute Jesus himself?**

● **How might you have persecuted Jesus in your own life?**

● **What can you do to spread God's Word, rather than persecute Jesus?**

Have everyone sit in a circle on the floor and ask some group members to share their thoughts on how we might persecute Christ in our lives and what we can do to spread his Word instead. After the discussion, lead the group in a prayer similar to this:

> Lord, we have persecuted you just as Saul did, and we ask your forgiveness. Fill us with your Holy Spirit so we, too, may be your disciples and share your Word with those who don't know you. Lead us as your chosen instruments to carry your name to all people. Amen.

If you would like to use this experience as a commissioning, lead your group in planning a mission or outreach experience to carry out in the next few weeks or months.

Scripture: Acts 10:34-48

Theme: The Holy Spirit

Experience: In this **creative writing experience**, teenagers will imagine

Handout

Saul's Conversion

(based on Acts 9:1-20)

*(**Soldiers** are standing around, watching and listening to Saul.)*

Saul: *(Stomping back and forth, angry, with a mean look on his face)* I'll kill those people who call themselves Christians—every last one of them—men and women. Who was this Jesus that they should follow him? No one of any importance—but something has to be done about this rabble! I know what I have to do. I'll go to the high priest and get letters to take to the synagogues in Damascus so I can arrest these Christians and take them as prisoners to Jerusalem! That'll crush them once and for all! Soldiers, come! Let's go to Damascus!

*(**Saul** sets out on his journey to Damascus, walking along the road with a few **soldiers**. Suddenly he covers his head with his arms and falls to the ground.)*

Saul: Ooww! That light hurts my eyes. Who's doing that?

Jesus: *(A voice from offstage)* "Saul, Saul, why do you persecute me?"

Saul: "Who are you, Lord?"

Jesus: "I am Jesus, whom you are persecuting. Now get up and go into the city, and you will be told what you must do."

*(**Saul** covers his eyes with his hand, since he cannot see, and the Soldier leads him by the other hand as if going to the city. Then **Saul** sits in a chair and some of his **disciples** sit around him on the floor.)*
*(**Ananias** stands on the other side of the stage, away from Saul.)*

Saul: It's been three days now, and I'm still blind. I can't eat anything. I can't drink anything. I can't see anything. What's happening to me?

Jesus: *(Speaking from offstage to Ananias)* "Ananias, go to the house of Judas on Straight Street, and ask for a man from Tarsus named Saul."

Ananias: "Lord, I have heard many reports about this man and all the harm he has done to your saints in Jerusalem. And he has come here with authority from the chief priests to arrest all who call on your name."

Jesus: *(Forcefully)* "Go! This man is my chosen instrument to carry my name before the Gentiles and their kings and before the people of Israel. I will show him how much he must suffer for my name."

*(**Ananias** walks over to where **Saul** is sitting and pretends to open a door and walk into the house.)*

Ananias: *(Places his hands on Saul's head.)* "Brother Saul, the Lord—Jesus, who appeared to you on the road as you were coming here—has sent me so that you may see again and be filled with the Holy Spirit."

Saul: *(Excitedly)* The scales have fallen from my eyes! I can see again! Will you baptize me, Ananias? I want to be a Christian and follow Jesus, my Lord.

*(**Saul** kneels as **Ananias** pretends to baptize him. When Ananias has finished, **Saul** pretends to eat some food, then lies down to rest for a minute.)*

Saul: *(Jumping up)* Who is coming with me? We're going to the synagogues to preach. I want every man and woman to know that Jesus is the Son of God! *(Walks offstage, leading the **disciples**.)*

what it was like to experience the Holy Spirit when Peter spoke to the Gentiles.

Preparation: You'll need Bibles, paper, and pens or pencils.

Worship

Say: **We're going to experience what it might have been like for the early Christians to experience the Holy Spirit. I'm going to read you a story from Acts 10:34-48, and I'd like you to listen carefully. Focus especially on what you think the early Christians may have been tasting, seeing, smelling, touching, and hearing. You may want to close your eyes as you listen.**

Read Acts 10:34-48 aloud with inflection and drama. When you've finished, give each person a Bible, a piece of paper, and a pencil or pen. Have young people write a few notes about what they think the early Christians were experiencing with each of their senses.

Have teenagers form pairs, and say:

Now I'd like you to write a first-person, eyewitness account with your partner of what it would have been like to be in the room with the early Christians. Start your account with a paraphrase of Peter's words about what it means to be a Christian, and then describe the Holy Spirit's presence. Use all five senses in your account.

After about five minutes, have pairs present their accounts to the group.

Scripture: Acts 13:44-52

Theme: Sharing faith

Experience: In this creative writing experience and prayer of thanksgiving, teenagers will express their appreciation to others for sharing their faith.

Preparation: You'll need Bibles, colorful writing paper, pens or pencils, and decorative stickers.

Worship

Read Acts 13:44-52 aloud. Summarize the important points in the passage.

Say: **Paul and Barnabas tried to preach the gospel to the Jews first but were rejected. They then preached to the Gentiles, to whom God gave the faith to believe. Many of them became Christians. Then Paul and Barnabas were driven out of the area. As they left, they shook the dust from their feet. In spite of these discouraging events, Paul and Barnabas were filled with joy and the Holy Spirit.**

Instead of becoming bitter or feeling sorry for themselves, Paul and Barnabas saw the situation from God's perspective. They rejoiced that

all those Gentiles had become Christians. They were filled with joy that comes only from a supernatural work of the Holy Spirit. True, everything seemed against them, but they were able to see past all the negative events. They had been called by God to preach the good news of Jesus' resurrection, and by God's power they wouldn't stop.

Give each person a Bible, a piece of colorful writing paper, a pen or pencil, and a decorative sticker. Instruct each teenager to locate a verse that has special meaning to him or her and serves as a reminder of what it means to know Christ. If teenagers need help on this, you may want to suggest such verses as Romans 6:23; Romans 10:9-10; Galatians 2:20; Philippians 3:7-11; and 1 Timothy 6:11-12.

Encourage each person to think of someone who shared the good news of Jesus with him or her, such as a parent, a pastor, a youth leader, or a friend. Then have teenagers write thank you letters to those people. Tell them to include the verses they found. When the letters are finished, instruct teenagers to fold the papers into thirds, securing them with decorative stickers.

Have teenagers sit in a circle. Tell them about someone who shared the good news of Jesus with you, and offer a prayer of thanksgiving for that person. Then have teenagers take turns offering up prayers of thanksgiving for the people their thank you letters are addressed to.

As teenagers leave, remind them to hand out or mail their letters at the next opportunity.

Scripture: Acts 17:22-31

Theme: God's revelation

Experience: In this **artistic experience** and **musical experience**, teenagers will recognize ways God has revealed himself to people through creation.

Preparation: You'll need newspapers; acrylic paints; paintbrushes; paper towels; Bibles; clay flowerpots; assorted cassettes or CDs of Christian music; a cassette or CD player; clear acrylic spray; potting soil; and assorted indoor plants such as flowers, cactuses, small vines, and leafy plants.

Before the experience, cover a table or an area of the floor with newspapers. Set out enough acrylic paints and paintbrushes for everyone. Make plenty of paper towels available for cleanup.

Worship

Read Acts 17:22-31 aloud. After reading the passage, say:

Notice how Paul took advantage of the Athenians' pagan religious beliefs to share his faith in Christ. He could have condemned them and told them how far off-target their beliefs were. Instead, Paul wisely bridged a gap to these non-Christians. Instead of insulting them, he commended their desire to be religious. Then he taught them about God.

Ask:

● How do Christians normally treat those who have different beliefs?

● What are some ways we can use the interest others have in religion to share our faith in Christ?

Reread verses 24-27 aloud.

Say: **Paul also recognized that God has made himself known to all people. The created world around us speaks of the presence and power of God. And our inner conscience tells us of God's existence. God has made sure every man, woman, and child can believe.**

Give each person a clay flowerpot. Instruct teenagers to use the acrylic paints and paintbrushes to decorate the flowerpots. Encourage them to be creative and to decorate the flower pots with designs that represent some ways God reveals himself to people, designs such as trees, flowers, stars, and hearts.

While the paint is drying, have teenagers sit in a circle. Distribute a variety of musical CDs or cassettes, and have them look through the music and choose songs that remind them of how God has made himself known to people. Spend some time listening to those songs together.

When the paint is dry, spray the flowerpots with clear acrylic spray. Then have teenagers choose plants, place them in potting soil in their pots, water the plants, and take them home.

Romans

Scripture: Romans 3:1-28

Theme: Atonement

Experience: In this act of commitment, creative writing experience, and prayer of confession, teenagers will talk with God about their unworthiness and their faith response.

Preparation: You'll need a photocopy of the "At-one-ment" handout (p. 24) for each person and Bibles

Worship

Give each person a copy of the "At-one-ment" handout and a Bible. Direct teenagers to sit as far from one another as space allows and complete the handouts on their own. As teenagers write, walk through the room and quietly invite each person to ask you a question about any of the statements on the handout.

After youth complete their handouts, invite each person to share one sentence from what he or she wrote. Affirm teenagers as they share.

Then ask:

- **What would happen if God just let us get away with sin?**
- **Why is getting rid of sin a critical task?**
- **How does at-one-ment with God make you want to be good?**

Pray together, thanking God for both loving us and taking sin seriously.

Scripture: Romans 5:1-19

Theme: Commitment to Jesus

Experience: In this **act of commitment**, teenagers will contemplate their relationship with Christ and have an opportunity to make a commitment to Jesus.

Preparation: You'll need a video camera, a videotape, a TV, a VCR, Bibles, newsprint, markers, tape or tacks, a cassette or CD of soft music, and a cassette or CD player.

Before the experience, videotape interviews with five or six people. Ask them, "What does it mean to become a Christian?"

Worship

Have teenagers form groups of four. Give each group a piece of newsprint and markers, then start the videotape. Show the first interview, then stop the tape.

Say: **I'd like you to discuss whether you agree with this person's answer and then write down your response.**

When groups have discussed and written their responses, show the next interview. Then stop the tape again. Continue this until all the interviews have been shown and groups have had a chance to discuss and record their responses to each interview. When you've finished this process, have each group join another group to form a group of eight. Have groups of eight discuss their responses to each video segment.

When all groups have shared, have teenagers form four equal groups.

Then say: **In your group, I'd like you to read Romans 5:1-19 aloud.**

Handout

At-One-Ment

Open your Bible to Romans 3:1-28. This is a passage about atonement, an experience with God that can be understood as "at-one-ment." It means having a relationship with God because your sin is forgiven.

Read Romans 3:1-28. Then complete the sentences below as a prayer to God. You'll be asked to share one sentence with the group later. The rest will be private.

God, I know I can be at one with you because…

It's amazing that you want to be at one with me even after I've done and thought bad things. But after I read Romans 3:1-18, I realize we all do wrong. If a verse were added after verse 18 to describe my wrongs, it would say…

I want to be perfect to please you, but, according to Romans 3:19-20, that's not possible. Your laws make me conscious of this sin in my life…

Since I can't become perfect on my own, I'll trust you to make me right with you (Romans 3:21-26). When I think about the fact that you both love me as I am and will help me to become better, I…

Because you love me and because you're perfect, I'll let you make me good (Romans 3:27-28). I'll let my goodness be a worship to you. One way I want to start doing the right thing is…

This is a passage that describes our need for deliverance from sin and God's response to that need. There's a lot in this passage, and it can be difficult to understand, so I'd like you to read it carefully and work together to understand its meaning.

After groups have read the passage, give each group another piece of newsprint, and redistribute markers. Assign each group one of the following passages: Romans 5:1-11; Romans 5:12-14; Romans 5:15-17; and Romans 5:18-19.

Have each group create a cartoon that represents the significance of its assigned passage. When groups have created their cartoons, have them post the cartoons in order on a wall in your meeting area.

Say: **This passage helps us see that sin was brought into the world through Adam. It also helps us understand that eternal life was brought into the world through Jesus. It makes it clear that Jesus died for us while we were spiritually dead in our sins. But Jesus' death on our behalf is something we must respond to. And we respond to it by confessing our sins to God and accepting Jesus' death for our sins.**

Let's spend some time considering how we might respond to this Scripture passage. Perhaps you want to consider making a faith commitment to Jesus for the first time. Maybe you want to spend some time praying for people who don't have a relationship with Jesus. Or maybe you just want to commit to find out more about what it means to be a Christian. Spend the next few minutes thinking or silently praying about a commitment you might be ready to make.

Play some soft music, and allow teenagers to sit in silence for a few minutes. Then close the meeting with a short prayer. After the prayer, make yourself available to talk with students who want to make a commitment to Jesus or find out more about what it means to be a Christian.

Scripture: Romans 6:1-12

Theme: Grace

Experience: In this **artistic experience, creative reading,** and **dramatic presentation,** teenagers will understand more about God's grace.

Preparation: You'll need Bibles, index cards, fine-tip markers, scissors, and a photocopy of the "Good News Credit Report" handout (p. 27) for each person.

Worship

Have teenagers form groups of four. (If the group is small, teenagers can form pairs or trios.) Give each group a Bible, an index card, markers, and a pair of scissors.

Romans

Have a person in each group read Romans 6:1-12 aloud. Then have teenagers discuss the following questions in their groups. Tell groups to be prepared to share their insights with the other groups. Ask:

● What does it mean to be "dead to sin"?

● How would you describe God's grace?

Say: **This is kind of a tough passage. Let's start at the beginning.** Ask:

● What does the first verse of this passage mean to you?

● Do you think that the more we sin, the more grace we receive? Explain.

Say: **The first verse is asking if we should sin more in order to receive more grace, or forgiveness, from God. The second verse answers the question with a big "No way!" God's grace covers our sins, but that doesn't mean it's OK to keep on sinning just because we know God will forgive us. Think of it as a credit card. Just because the credit is available doesn't mean you should run up a big bill.**

In your group, create a spiritual credit card with your index card and markers. Then create a commercial to entice credit card holders to run up their bills. For example, you might say, "C'mon, what are you waiting for? You can do anything you want, with the City of Sin Bank Card! Free grace period available!" Make sure everyone in your group has a part in the commercial.

Give groups about five minutes to create their cards and commercials, then have groups present their commercials. Applaud each group's presentation.

Give each group member a copy of the "Good News Credit Report" handout. Have groups assign each member at least one part until all the parts are assigned. Then have teenagers read the script aloud in each group. Encourage teenagers to worship God as they're reading their scripts, expressing thanks for God's grace.

When groups have finished reading the script, say:

Sometimes people cut up their credit cards so they can't run up big bills. They don't even want to be tempted to use the credit card. Let's cut up these spiritual credit cards to show we don't want to be tempted by sin. Pass the card and the scissors around your group. As each person cuts off a piece of the card, mention a way you'll resist sin this week.

Have teenagers take home their credit card pieces to remind them of their commitments.

● **Good News Credit Report** ●

(based on Romans 6:1-12)

Assign these roles within your group:
- ● Credit Bureau President
- ● Debtor #1
- ● Debtor #2
- ● Debtor #3

Credit Bureau President: (*Looking at watch*) Next?…Yes, yes, what is it? Step ahead, please; there's a long line of debtors behind you!

Debtor #1: (*hesitantly*) Well, you see, I have a slight problem. I, uh, well, I, um…

Credit Bureau President: Out with it! Can't you see I'm busy? We're short-staffed today, and I have more debtors than I can possibly handle. Spit it out, or step out of line!

Debtor #1: (*In a rush*) OK, well, I know I'm supposed to be dead to sin and all that, but there's this one sin that keeps appearing on my credit report, and I don't know what to do about it. I'm really sorry every time I commit this sin, and I'm really trying to stop, and I was wondering if you could help me. I feel so guilty!

Credit Bureau President: Of course, *I* can't help you—I'm just a government employee. But I'll see if *he* can. Just a moment.

(*Pretends to talk on phone.*) Sir? I have one here who seems to understand the whole concept but still needs a little help in the execution…Yes, sir…Very well, sir. (*Hangs up phone.*)

The Master says to remind you that each time you've asked for forgiveness for this particular sin, the sin has been erased on your report in the main office. That report you have there is outdated. To help you maintain a clean credit report, the Master suggests consulting your owner's manual—you know, the book with the cross on the front that's collecting dust on your shelf. Also, he says he's willing to speak with you personally on the special hot line he's set up. Dial 1-800-THE-CROSS. Next?

Handout

Debtor #2: (*Arrogantly*) Yeah, well, my report is all wrong! I happen to *know* that I have more grace coming to me than this thing says. I distinctly remember reading the clause when I first signed up—it was something about having grace abundantly. Now, I know that I've been sinning a lot lately, but that means I should have more grace, right? I want this changed!

Credit Bureau President: One moment, please. (*Picks up phone.*) Sir? Yes...we have another one here who completely misunderstands the grace clause. Yes...I'll try, sir. (*Hangs up, sighing.*) The Master says you have it backward. The goal is to require *less* grace, not more. The more you realize the price the Master paid to cover your debts, the fewer debts you should want to incur. It's really very simple. Next?

Debtor #3: (*Looking down.*) I have this report here. It's...uh...kind of long. (*Pretends to shuffle through lots of pages.*) I know there's probably nothing you can do to help me, but this friend of mine said the Master could consolidate my debts for me. She said he did it for her. Of course, her debts weren't nearly as bad as mine. I think my case is hopeless.

Credit Bureau President: (*Flipping through pages.*) Oh, my. This looks very bad. Very bad, indeed. I've known the Master to handle some pretty dire cases, but this looks very bad, indeed. Well, I'll see what I can do. (*Picks up phone.*) Sir? Sorry to trouble you again, but...(*covers mouth and whispers*) we have one here that even you'll agree...Oh, you have a copy?...I know, sir, but surely...Yes, I know he's repented, but if you'll just turn to page 27...What's that, sir? I can barely hear you...(*Rolls eyes impatiently.*) Sir, could you please ask the angels to rejoice a little less loudly?...Yes, sir...Very well. (*Sighs and hangs up phone.*) The Master says that your old self died on the cross with him, and I'm to issue you this clean credit rating. He'll be contacting you shortly. Next?

Scripture: Romans 8:6-17

Theme: Children of God

Experience: In this **creative movement** and **creative reading**, teenagers will pantomime the truth of Romans 8:6-17.

Preparation: You'll need Bibles.

Worship

Because Romans 8:6-17 is full of contrasts and powerful truths, guide teenagers through a pantomime of it as worship to God. You may want to take them through these steps:

1. Remind teenagers that God is the audience, and encourage them to continually focus their attention on God as they pantomime.

2. Assign a portion of the passage to each person or to a group of people. The person or group should direct the other teenagers in the expression of the assigned passage.

Some sample verse divisions that form single scenes are 6, 7-8, 9a, 9b, 10, 11, 12, 13a, 13b, 14-15, 16, and 17. You can combine verses to accommodate fewer teenagers or teams. Give each person or group of people a few moments to consider how to portray the assigned passage.

For example, the student guiding verse 6 might guide teenagers to shape their bodies in ways that show contrasts between the mind of sinful man and the mind controlled by the Spirit. For the sinful man, teenagers might look arrogant and scornful and then die; for the mind controlled by the Spirit, they might adopt caring, peaceful stances.

3. Involve all teenagers in the acting process at the same time. Consider letting the first run-through be the actual worship rather than a practice.

4. Encourage teenagers to find unique ways to dramatize the difference between physical and spiritual life and physical and spiritual death. They'll do better than you'd ever dream.

5. Read the passage as teenagers pantomime it.

Following the pantomime, invite each young person to name something he or she liked about the dramatic presentation. Then invite teenagers to talk about ways they can dramatize the truth of this passage in their daily actions.

Scripture: Romans 8:22-30

Theme: Caring for each other

Experience: In this **prayer of intercession**, teenagers will demonstrate care for one another's pain.

Preparation: You'll need Bibles and foot-long strips of yarn in various colors.

Romans

Worship

Give each student as many foot-long strips of yarn as you have teenagers. For example, if you have ten teenagers, each teenager should get ten pieces of yarn. Provide a different color for each student if possible.

Have teenagers sit in a circle on the floor.

Say: **I'd like each person to name three experiences in his or her life that have caused pain. Some examples are a disability, the death of a beloved grandparent, a disease, and a struggle to understand a school subject. After one person has shared, we'll all give that person nonverbal expressions of our friendship by handing him or her a piece of yarn as we pray.**

After the first young person has had an opportunity to share three experiences, guide everyone else to give that person a yarn strip while silently praying for him or her. After everyone has given the young person a yarn strip, ask the person to the left of the sharing teenager to read Romans 8:26-27 aloud.

Repeat this process for each teenager so each person receives prayers represented by yarn strips and each hears Romans 8:26-27 read specifically for him or her.

When everyone has shared, suggest to the teenagers that they braid their yarn strips together as a symbol of their commitment to walk with one another through pain. Read Romans 8:28 aloud, and say:

Romans 8:28 doesn't mean we shouldn't feel sad when painful things happen. In fact, we can help live Romans 8:28—the goodness God continues to give—by walking with friends through the sadness.

You may want to encourage the teenagers to discuss specific ways they can walk with one another through pain.

Scripture: Romans 8:31-39

Theme: God's presence

Experience: In this act of praise and creative reading, teenagers will celebrate God's constant presence.

Preparation: You'll need five pieces of poster board, a marker, six photocopies of the "Romans 8:31-39 Praise" script (p. 31), and a Bible.

Before the experience, make five cue cards on poster board. Write these phrases on the cue cards: "No one!" "He will!" "Hooray!" "Only Jesus!" and "No!" Find five volunteers to hold the cue cards and one to act as the narrator.

Romans 8:31-39 Praise

"What, then, shall we say in response to this? If God is for us, who can be against us?

NO ONE!

He who did not spare his own Son, but gave him up for us all—how will he not also, along with him, graciously give us all things?

HE WILL!

Who will bring any charge against those whom God has chosen?

NO ONE!

It is God who justifies.

HOORAY!

Who is he that condemns?

ONLY JESUS

Christ Jesus, who died—more than that, who was raised to life—is at the right hand of God and is also interceding for us.

HOORAY!

Who shall separate us from the love of Christ?

NO ONE!

Shall trouble or hardship or persecution or famine or nakedness or danger or sword?

NO!

As it is written:

'For your sake we face death all day long;

we are considered as sheep to be slaughtered.'

No, in all things we are more than conquerors through him who loved us.

HOORAY!

For I am convinced that neither death nor life,

NO!

neither angels nor demons,

NO!

neither the present nor the future,

NO!

nor any powers,

NO!

neither height nor depth,

NO!

nor anything else in all creation,

NO!

will be able to separate us from the love of God that is in Christ Jesus our Lord."

HOORAY!

1 Corinthians

Worship

Give each of the five cue-card holders a copy of the "Romans 8:31-39 Praise" script, and have the cue-card holders sit across the front of the room. Have the rest of the teenagers sit facing them.

Say: **In a moment we'll listen to a Bible passage. At certain points during the reading, these people will hold up cue cards. When you see a cue card go up, yell out what's written on it. For example, if the cue card says "Hooray!" everyone should yell "Hooray!" in unison.**

Give the narrator a copy of the "Romans 8:31-39 Praise" script and ask him or her to read the script aloud. As the narrator reads the script, prompt the cue-card holders to hold up their cue cards as the script indicates. Lead the rest of the group in responding to the passage according to cue.

After the reading, read Romans 8:38-39 aloud.

Then say: **Romans 8:38-39 are perhaps the most powerful verses in Romans 8 because they assure us that God *always* goes with us.**

Lead youth in repeating verses 38 and 39 three times in unison, each time trying to say the verses from memory. Call for volunteers to try to recite them as a testimony to God's continuing presence. Don't be surprised if they insert the cues while quoting the verses. The cues have helped them remember the verses.

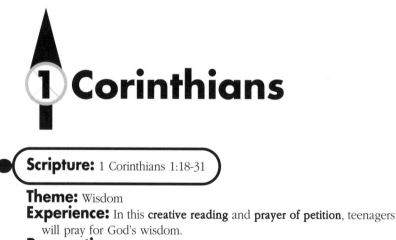

①Corinthians

Scripture: 1 Corinthians 1:18-31

Theme: Wisdom

Experience: In this **creative reading** and **prayer of petition**, teenagers will pray for God's wisdom.

Preparation: You'll need a diamond ring or another obviously precious object, a saltine cracker, a Bible, a CD or cassette of soft instrumental music, and a CD or cassette player.

1 Corinthians

Worship

Place a diamond ring (or another obviously precious object) and a saltine cracker on a table top. Ask teenagers to line up in front of the object they think they'd be wisest to choose if they could have either object. Give no more information about the choices.

When everyone has selected an object, ask teenagers to stay in their lines while you tell them a story.

> Say: **It was considered the best ship in the cruise company's line. They said it was an unsinkable ship. A ship in which every engineering flaw had been solved. The Titanic had gone down because of an iceberg. The Maine had blown up. But the Good Ship Lollipop? Unsinkable.**
>
> **At least, they said that it was unsinkable until it sank. Which it did. Like a rock.**
>
> **But you were able to get into a tiny lifeboat that bobbed away from the sinking vessel. And with you, to sustain you throughout your stay on the lifeboat, was the one object you in your wisdom had selected to take with you.**

At this point, ask if anyone would like to change lines. When everyone who wants to move has done so, continue with the story.

> **Just moments after the Good Ship Lollipop sank, a large ship steamed into view, making straight for you. As the ship grew close, you could see the crew—a leering, peg-legged crew of pirates! The pirate captain looked down on you. He wore an eye patch. The pirate's pet parrot, which clung to his left shoulder, also wore an eye patch. And the pirate called down, "Aye, matey! We'll take you aboard if you've got something worth havin'! What've ye got I might treasure?"**

At this point, ask if anyone would like to change lines. When everyone who wants to move has done so, continue with the story.

> **The pirate captain continued, "And don't be offerin' me no gold or fancy jewelry! I've got plenty of that in the hold below. Use it for ballast, I do. Give me somethin' fer Polly here. We've been at sea for almost a full year now, and Polly's hankerin' somethin' fierce for her favorite treat. I'll bring ye on board and save your worthless life if yer carryin' somethin' for my pet parrot. And what does Polly want? Why, ye filthy landlubber, Polly wants a cracker!"**

Ask teenagers to sit in a circle. Ask:

● If you'd known the entire story, would you have made the first choice you made? Why or why not?

● When have you wished you'd known the entire story before you made a choice?

1 Corinthians

Say: **We seldom have the entire story when we have to make a decision. For example, some of you may be wondering where to go to college or whether to go at all. It would be great to know how your life will turn out before you have to make that decision.**

You don't have all the information about your own life, let alone anyone else's. But you know the one who *does* know the entire story: God. Will you trust God to guide your decisions? That's the beginning of wisdom: trusting the only one who knows the future and loves you.

Ask teenagers to form pairs and find a space in the room where they can talk softly and not disturb others. Ask partners to sit knee to knee, eye to eye.

Say: **Psalm 111 says, "The fear of the Lord is the beginning of wisdom; all who follow his precepts have good understanding." The word "fear" doesn't mean trembling in fright; it means *reverence*. Wisdom begins with worshiping God and knowing God's Word.**

Read 1 Corinthians 1:18-31 aloud. Then say:

With your partner, please discuss a decision you're facing. It can be as personal and risky or as safe as you wish; please decide together to keep everything you say private. You and your partner will seek God's wisdom together in prayer.

Begin by praying aloud for what will happen in the next ten minutes— that honest sharing will happen and that God's wisdom will be given freely to those who wish to receive and act on it. When you've finished praying, announce that pairs will have ten minutes to share and you'll give updates as time passes. Suggest that whoever shares first take no longer than three minutes and that partners pray together for a few minutes before the second partner shares.

Play soft instrumental music as pairs are sharing. Give gentle five-, three-, and one-minute countdowns.

Scripture: 1 Corinthians 2:1-11

Theme: Servanthood

Experience: In this **act of commitment** and **dramatic presentation**, teenagers will offer themselves as imperfect servants of God.

Preparation: You'll need one photocopy of "The Island Bridge" script (p. 35), a stack of newspaper pages, a Bible, and three photocopies of the "Bridge Builder" handout (p. 38).

Before the experience, ask a student to act as the narrator for the dramatic presentation. Give that person "The Island Bridge" script so he or she can become familiar with it beforehand. Set up a chair on one side

The Island Bridge

A certain island sat in the middle of a broad river. The people on the island were completely self-sufficient and seldom left the island. The islanders ate fish they caught in the wide, graceful river. They lived in houses built with the abundant lumber harvested on the island. Their farms produced ample vegetables. Islanders were born, grew up, fell in love, married, raised children, and then died on the island.

For generations, the islanders lived peacefully. And then one morning, the only two islanders who had telephones got calls from upstream.

A terrible storm was dumping thousands of gallons of water a minute on the island. A dam was bulging and cracking. It was just a matter of time until the dam would burst and a deadly, surging flood would completely engulf the island—and the islanders.

The only solution was to get the islanders across the bridge and off the island. Except there *wasn't* a bridge. So few islanders had wanted to leave that there had never been a reason to build a bridge.

But clearly there was a reason now—and no time to waste.

So one islander, Frank, leapt into action. He ran to his desk and pulled out a textbook about the engineering principles behind bridge building. Frank dashed off an application letter to a nearby engineering college so he could sharpen the skills he'd need to make the bridge a model of bridge building, a bridge that would last for generations.

Frank read through the island newspaper to determine whether he would need the support of political leaders to get a bridge-building project approved. He quickly jotted himself a note to write a letter to the National Association of Bridge-Building Professionals to ask for grant money to fund the bridge. And he called the Environmental Impact Department to see if building the bridge would threaten any endangered plants or animals that might live along the riverbank.

Lynn also leapt into action.

First she gathered the islanders together. Lynn explained the phone call she had received and asked everyone to help build a bridge. She told the islanders that the bridge may not *look* like what everyone expected or be exactly *where* everyone thought a bridge should go, but the bridge would *get them all safely off the island.*

Motivated, each islander grabbed a sheet of bridge-building material. Each islander laid down his or her sheet to create a bridge leading off the island. Then the islanders walked across to safety.

Handout

Only Frank was left behind because he was too busy becoming an expert bridge builder to actually help build one—or even to walk across it when it was time.

So after the flood waters receded and the bridge was still standing, they named it the Frank Memorial Bridge. It's still there—and islanders are still using it to reach safety.

of the area of your room that will become the "stage."

Ask three students to act as readers for the "Bridge Builder" handout, and assign one reading segment to each reader. Give handouts to the students beforehand so they can practice reading.

Worship

Ask for two volunteers—one male and one female—to be actors. Tell the male actor his name is Frank, and the female her name is Lynn. Tell Frank and Lynn to act out the story as the narrator reads it.

Say: **Jesus told a lot of parables—stories with a deeper meaning that open windows of insight onto spiritual issues. Our actors will now help you experience a parable; then we'll discuss it. Our actors will act out the story as our narrator tells it...and you have a part too. You're the islanders in our story, and here are your props.**

Point to the stack of newspaper pages, but don't distribute them.

Be ready to act when you hear your part.

Have the actor playing Frank sit in the chair on the stage. Have Lynn stand facing the audience on the other side of the stage. Then have the narrator read "The Island Bridge" script aloud. When he or she reads, "Each islander grabbed a sheet of bridge-building material," prompt the group to grab sheets of newspaper from the stack.

When your group has finished acting out the parable, gather everyone in a circle. Ask a volunteer to read 1 Corinthians 2:1-5 aloud.

Then ask Reader 1 to read the first segment of the "Bridge Builder" handout. When he or she has finished reading, ask teenagers to confess their imperfections to God in silent prayer.

Ask Reader 2 to read the second segment of the "Bridge Builder" handout. When he or she has finished reading, ask teenagers to offer one-word prayers about bridges that need building: the name of a friend who needs to hear about Jesus, someone who's trapped by anger or fear, or someone who's isolated by loneliness.

Ask Reader 3 to read the third segment of the "Bridge Builder" handout. When he or she has finished reading, ask teenagers to take one step forward if they wish to silently affirm this prayer.

Then say:

You're called to help others reach safe ground over the bridge of Christ. Are you totally prepared for this task? Absolutely not. Will you *ever* be totally prepared? Absolutely not. And that's OK—because your job is to give what you have in service to Christ. He'll use what you have now, as imperfect as you are. And as you grow in your faith, God will continue to use you.

Handout

BRIDGE BUILDER

Reader 1: The Apostle Paul was far from perfect. He was sometimes impatient. He had tracked down and imprisoned Christians. He called himself "worst among sinners." Yet you used him, God, to be a bridge builder.

Reader 2: We know you still need bridge builders, God. People who will build bridges between people who are angry with each other. Between you and those who need to hear about you. Between ourselves and others. Bring to our minds bridges you want built.

Reader 3: We offer ourselves as bridge builders, God. We confess that, like Paul, we're imperfect. But we know *you're* perfect. We confess we're inadequate. But *you're* adequate. We confess we're not sure what to do. But *you* know what to do. We offer ourselves, and we believe you'll use us, God.

1 Corinthians

Scripture: 1 Corinthians 8:1-13

Theme: Selflessness

Experience: In this **act of commitment** and **creative reading**, teenagers will recognize that Jesus set aside his rights as God to serve us.

Preparation: You'll need a large candle, matches, one small candle for each person, a photocopy of the "He Understands" script (p. 40), and a Bible.

Before the experience, darken your meeting area as much as possible.

Worship

Have youth sit in a circle. Light the large candle, and place the lit candle in the center of the circle. Give each person an unlit candle.

Ask confident volunteers to take turns reading segments of the "He Understands" script as it's passed around the circle. Avoid forcing teenagers to read aloud—it can be embarrassing for struggling readers, and teenagers may be more concerned about performance than experiencing the activity.

When teenagers have finished reading the script, say:

> Jesus set aside his rights as creator of the universe to serve us. He traded the glory of heaven for a borrowed manger in Bethlehem. He willingly suffered and endured the cross even though it wasn't a debt he owed. We owed it, but Jesus paid it. And his love is a light that shines.

Read 1 Corinthians 8:1-13 aloud. Then say:

> We have rights too. But insisting on our rights may not be healthy for other believers. Something we do may be right, but it may still cause a weaker Christian who looks up to us to question his or her faith. Here in our circle, let's identify some of those things.

Encourage teenagers to brainstorm, then say:

> The question that faces us is this: Are we willing to love others enough to *not* insist on our rights to do these things if they cause other Christians to question God? The goal isn't to let weaker brothers and sisters stay weaker; they need to grow. But until they do, are we willing to pay a price to encourage them?
>
> If you're willing to set aside one of your rights this week to encourage others, join me in sharing in this light that draws us together.

Light your candle from the center candle, and hold your candle as you offer a sentence prayer of dedication to serving others. Then pass the flame around the circle. Encourage teenagers to join you in offering sentence prayers as they hold their lit candles.

Handout

He Understands

It was the day of judgment, and a vast throng of people waited before God's throne. But they didn't wait in silence.

A crowd of broken men and women shouted toward God's shining throne, "We lived and died homeless, shifted from shelter to shelter until disease and exposure claimed us. You have all of heaven at your feet. How can you know how life and apathy ground us down? You have no idea what it's like to pass unnoticed in a city street, to have people shift their eyes to keep from seeing you. You've never been homeless for even a minute. There is no justice in your judging us because you don't know how we lived or died."

Millions of Jews stood in tattered rags, yellow stars sewn on their chests. They took up the shouting. "We want to know who you are to judge us! We were torn from our homes and shoved like cattle into frozen boxcars. We were marched naked into concentration-camp gas chambers and slaughtered. You who live in splendor cannot possibly know what we have endured!"

Down a long, golden street limped thousands of thin, emaciated people, many of them children. Their hollow eyes shone fiercely. "And us," they shouted. "How can you understand us? We who called out for food and water and received none? We who were born to famine and died staring at empty skies and empty hands? You know nothing of our lives. You who are surrounded by plenty have no right to judge us. What would *you* do for food if you felt hunger tearing at your stomach?"

Across the great plain before God's throne stood the homeless, the poor, those who had died unjustly and without being avenged, the defenseless, the downtrodden. And their voices rose up in a chorus of indignation and pain. Who was God to presume to understand them? How could anyone who had never suffered even *pretend* to understand? They stood and shook their fists, screaming.

Then from the right hand of God walked a familiar figure. His hands were scarred. His robe was bloodied. He carried a crown of thorns.

Those who had suffered quit screaming, then quietly sat down. Those who had lived without homes joined them. Those who had endured hunger, torture, and death at the hands of evil sat down. All across the great plain the crowd grew silent and still.

God did understand after all.

1 Corinthians

Scripture: 1 Corinthians 9:16-27

Theme: Spiritual growth

Experience: In this **artistic experience** and **prayer of intercession**, teenagers will set goals for their own spiritual growth.

Preparation: You'll need a container of modeling dough for every two people, one extra container of modeling dough, Bibles, a CD or cassette of soft instrumental music, and a CD or cassette player.

The night before the experience, place the extra container of modeling dough in a freezer.

Worship

Ask teenagers to form pairs, and give each pair a container of modeling dough, giving one pair the container of frozen modeling dough. Ask teenagers not to open their modeling dough yet.

If it's important that you reuse the modeling dough later, announce at the beginning of this activity that you'll need it back with one color in each container.

Say: **One biblical image portrays God as a potter and God's people as clay. God can mold us into useful containers. In the next sixty seconds, open your modeling dough container, and divide the contents between you so that each person can create a useful container of some sort. Go.**

After sixty seconds, ask teenagers to show their creations. Affirm each person's work. When the teenagers who struggled with the frozen modeling dough display their work, ask:

What happened here?

Let the teenagers share their frustration, then say:

I gave this pair a surprise: *frozen* **modeling dough. There wasn't much they could do with it!**

Replace the frozen container with a usable one, and ask pairs to form groups of four to discuss the following questions:

● **Think of yourself as clay. How pliable are you in God's hands?**

● **What's one way God has shaped your life in the past year?**

● **If you could ask God to shape you in some way, what would you ask for?**

Ask a volunteer in each group to read aloud 1 Corinthians 9:24-27. Say:

Paul advocates an intentional faith, one in which spiritual growth comes from living a disciplined life. Most of us by nature are not disciplined when it comes to our spiritual lives. We'll discipline our bodies so we can make a sports team and discipline our minds so we

1 Corinthians

can pass a test, but what about our spiritual lives? We mostly wander around and hope for the best.

Take a few minutes to create a small sculpture of a step you could take to have a more disciplined, intentional spiritual life, a next step that will bring you closer to God.

Play soft music as teenagers work. When everyone has finished, ask teenagers to share with their groups what their sculptures mean.

Say: **As you describe what your sculpture means, also share what that next step would look like. For example, if you sculpted a person praying, are you willing to pray more? When? What would you pray about? As specifically as possible, suggest a tiny next step God can use to mold you.**

After teenagers share, say:

A growing spiritual life is a partnership. It takes God's grace, but it *also* takes our effort. Let's pray for one another to have the discipline to take the "next step." Please take turns praying for each person in your group. When you've finished praying for one another, please pray silently for yourself. Honestly decide whether you're willing to take the next small step. And before you leave your group, select one other person for whom you'll pray in the coming week.

Leader Tip

On a tight budget? Create your own modeling dough by combining one part salt to two parts flour. Add water and mix and knead the dough until it's stiff. Place in plastic baggies.

Be warned: The salt stings if anyone using the dough has an open wound on his or her hands.

When small groups have finished praying, close with a group prayer of dedication for the coming week. Ask God to mold your group as, together, you take next steps toward spiritual growth.

Scripture: 1 Corinthians 10:1-13

Theme: Wisdom

Experience: In this creative writing experience and sharing time, teenagers will write an instruction book for younger Christians.

Preparation: You'll need Bibles, paper, colored markers, pens or pencils, and staplers.

Before the experience, decide on a group of younger Christians in your church to whom the teenagers in your class could give the benefit of their wisdom. Your class will create a book of warnings and wisdom for the younger group.

1 Corinthians

Worship

Have teenagers form groups of three or four, and make sure each person has a Bible. Have a person in each group read aloud 1 Corinthians 10:1-13 as the other teenagers follow along. After teenagers finish reading, have them discuss the following questions in their groups. After each question, ask volunteers to share their groups' insights and discoveries. Ask:

● Why would Paul warn the Corinthians to look back at the Israelites' history?

● How can things that happened in the past help us face the future?

● What's one mistake you made in the past that taught you a valuable lesson?

Give each group a supply of paper, markers, and pens or pencils.

Say: **We can use our own experiences to help other Christians grow in their faith. One way to do that is to create a book of wisdom for younger Christians in our church. Each of you will create a page for the book by relating something you've learned about knowing, serving, and following God. You might write words of encouragement, warning, or praise based on a lesson you've experienced in your own life.**

You can present your words of wisdom in any way you choose. You can draw a cartoon or a sign, write a short story or poem, or simply relate what happened to you and what you learned from it. Try to relate your wisdom in a way the younger Christians will be able to understand. After we've compiled our book, we'll make copies of it and present the books to the younger Christians.

When teenagers have finished creating their pages, have them share what they've written. Let students agree on a title for the book and work together to create a cover. Then collect and photocopy the pages, and let teenagers collate and staple the pages together to form books.

Arrange for your group to meet with a group of younger Christians to present their books. Let each teenager present his or her page to the younger class and explain its significance. Then present the books to the younger students, and close with a group prayer.

Scripture: 1 Corinthians 11:23-26

Theme: The future

Experience: In this **celebration of the Lord's Supper,** teenagers will prepare their own bread and consider how God uses the loaf and cup to bring them strength for the future. This idea works best at a retreat or another gathering that lasts at least three hours.

1 Corinthians

Persian Flat-Bread
(makes two loaves)

This bread recipe is often used in the area of the world where Jesus lived when he was on earth.

2 cups milk, scalded

2 tablespoons cooking oil

2 tablespoons molasses

2 tablespoons honey

2 teaspoons salt

1 teaspoon cinnamon

1 package yeast

¼ cup warm water (105 to 115 degrees Fahrenheit)

5½ cups whole wheat flour (approximately)

¼ cup milk (approximately)

¼ cup sesame seeds

Combine scalded milk, oil, molasses, honey, salt, and cinnamon. Cool to lukewarm. Dissolve yeast in warm water, and stir into milk mixture. Gradually stir in enough of the flour to make a stiff dough. Cover the bowl with a damp towel. Let the dough rise in a warm place for approximately 1 hour. Knead dough until smooth and elastic. Divide it in half and shape each half into a circle. Place on greased baking sheet, brush with milk, and sprinkle with sesame seeds. Let the dough rise for an additional 30 to 40 minutes. Bake in a 350-degree oven for 40 to 45 minutes.

Preparation: You'll need a Bible, ingredients for Persian Flat-Bread (see the recipe in the margin), serving plates, and grape juice either in a chalice or in small cups for individual service.

Before the experience, pick out some games or activities for teenagers to participate in while the bread is rising and baking, or plan a study of 1 Corinthians 11:23-26. If necessary, arrange for a member of the clergy to officiate the Lord's Supper at the appropriate time.

Worship

Have one teenager read 1 Corinthians 11:23-26 aloud. After the Scripture reading, ask: **What would it have been like to make the actual bread eaten by Jesus and his disciples at the Last Supper?**

Lead teenagers in making bread for the Lord's Supper, following the recipe in the margin. While the bread is rising and baking, lead teenagers in some games and activities or a study of 1 Corinthians 11:23-26.

When the bread is ready, prepare the elements of the Lord's Supper, and ask a teenager to read 1 Corinthians 11:23-26 aloud again. Have teenagers form pairs, and say:

When Jesus broke the bread and passed the cup to his disciples at the Last Supper, he knew he would soon be turned over to the authorities and crucified. Discuss with your partner whether you think Jesus knew the trials and punishment his disciples would face as they spread the good news about him after his death and resurrection. Explain your thoughts.

After one or two minutes, ask:

● **Why do you think, of all the possible things he could have chosen, Jesus chose a** loaf of bread and a cup as symbols by which people were to remember him?

● **In what ways does God use the Lord's Supper to bring us strength for** the future?

● **What area of your life do you need strength in right now?**

1 Corinthians

• How will the memory of the sacrifice Jesus made give you additional strength to face your future?

When pairs have finished discussing, partake of the Lord's Supper together.

After the Lord's Supper, say:

> Now share with your partner one way you will be strengthened today as a result of taking the Lord's Supper *in remembrance of Jesus*. Then say a silent prayer, asking for Christ's strength for the future.

Leader Tip

You can also use this worship experience as a service opportunity. Make an extra loaf of bread, and donate it to the church to use in celebrating the Lord's Supper. Another alternative is to make several loaves and then deliver them to shut-in members of the congregation.

Scripture: 1 Corinthians 12:1-11

Theme: Gifts and talents

Experience: In this **offering**, teenagers will celebrate God's special creation of each person, uniquely endowed with gifts for service to God.

Preparation: You'll need a Bible and several leaves from trees or plants. It doesn't matter whether they're dry or green. Make sure you have at least one leaf for every person.

Before the experience, ask participants to bring something that symbolizes or represents what they believe to be a special gift or talent God has given them. Set up a table at the front of the room.

Worship

Give each person a leaf. Ask a teenager to read 1 Corinthians 12:1-11 aloud.

Say: **Turn your attention to the leaf you're holding.**

Pause.

Study it for a moment.

Pause.

Look at its delicate veins.

Pause.

Notice its color.

Pause.

What does it feel like?

Pause.

Turn it over slowly, and look at its shape.

Pause.

The leaf in your hand is unique and different from any other leaf in the world because God made it that way. Think about how that leaf would have probably gone unobserved and unappreciated if you hadn't taken time to hold and observe it.

Pause.

In a way, people are a lot like that leaf. Each person is different, carefully created by God.

As I read the Bible passage to you again, close your eyes and think about the moment God created you.

Read only verses 4-6 and 11, pausing after each verse.

Say: **As a special offering, let's offer our special gifts and talents to God. One at a time, bring the item you brought with you to the front of the room. In a sentence or two, explain how that item symbolizes the special talent or gift God has given you. Then as an act of dedicating your talent to God, place your item on the table.**

After all the items have been brought forward, say a prayer of thanksgiving for the special talents and gifts God has given everyone.

Scripture: 1 Corinthians 12:12-27

Theme: Spiritual gifts

Experience: In this **artistic experience,** teenagers will show why every person in the body of Christ is equally valuable.

Preparation: You'll need Bibles, paper, scissors, pens or pencils, markers, and newsprint.

Before the experience, cut 8½ x 11 sheets of paper into thirds lengthwise. You'll need one strip of paper for each person.

Worship

Read 1 Corinthians 12:12-27 aloud as teenagers read along in their Bibles. Then give each person a strip of paper, and make pens or pencils and markers available to everyone.

Say: **1 Corinthians 12:12-27 is a wonderful example of God's great sense of humor. This passage also has a great message. I'd like you to draw a cartoon of 1 Corinthians 12:12-27 with at least six frames. For example, in one frame, you may draw a foot saying, "Because I am not a hand, I do not belong to the body" and running off by itself.**

If teenagers have trouble getting started, you may want to suggest that they divide the verses into cartoon frames this way: verses 12-13, verses 14-15, verse 16, verses 17-20, verses 21-25, and verses 26-27.

When everyone has finished creating a cartoon, ask teenagers to present their cartoons. As they do so, be sure to highlight a spiritual insight in each cartoon. Then ask:

● People belong to youth groups not because the group decides they belong, but because God gives each Christian a gift that group needs. God brings a variety of people into our group, and all of these people have something to offer the body of Christ. How is the way we treat people a way to worship God?

● How is accepting and living your giftedness a way to worship God?

● What specific action will you take to affirm each person's spiritual gift, including your own?

To cap this worship experience, lay out a sheet of newsprint. Help the teenagers work together to draw a comic strip that includes every member of the group as a way of offering themselves in unity to God.

Scripture: 1 Corinthians 13:1-13

Theme: Love

Experience: In this act of commitment, teenagers will pledge to love their friends.

Preparation: You'll need newsprint, a marker, masking tape, Bibles, chewing gum, a photocopy of the "Love-o-Meter" handout (p. 48) for each person, and pens or pencils.

Before the experience, write "the greatest gift I've ever received" on a piece of newsprint, and tape the newsprint to the wall.

Worship

Give each teenager a piece of chewing gum and say:

Chew this, and then form it into a representation of the greatest gift you've ever received. When you've done that, stick it to the newsprint on the wall.

Allow students time to chew their gum and make their shapes. When all the shapes are on the newsprint, ask teenagers to go to the newsprint one at a time and explain their shapes and the gift they represent.

Then say:

You've done an excellent job talking about the great gifts you've received. One of the greatest gifts we can give each other is love. In order to understand what love is, let's spend some time rating various acts of love.

Give each person a "Love-o-Meter" handout, and ask teenagers to rate

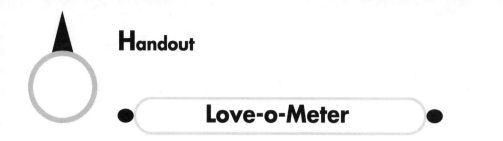

Handout

Love-o-Meter

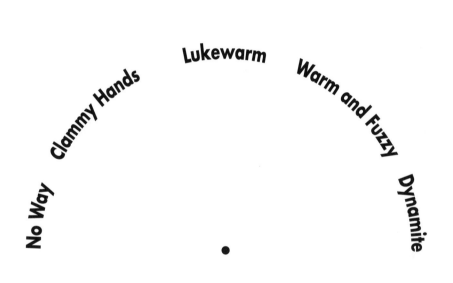

No Way

Clammy Hands

Lukewarm

Warm and Fuzzy

Dynamite

the following ways of showing love according to how much love is involved in each one.

Say: **I'll read a way to show love, and you'll draw an arrow from the center of your love-o-meter to the appropriate point on the love-o-meter.**

Read the following phrases, pausing after each one so teenagers can fill in their handouts:
- offering a helping hand
- giving a hug
- telling someone about Jesus
- getting married
- going to the prom
- giving someone money

Have teenagers form groups of three or four and share their responses. When they've shared, have groups read 1 Corinthians 13:1-13. Then ask:
- What did you notice about love in this passage?
- According to this passage, what does love look like?
- Why did Paul stress the importance of love? Explain.

Say: **One thing this passage points out is how important it is that we express and share our love. In fact, that's what's so neat about love. We get it from God; then we get to give it away. Now I'd like you to think of a way you can commit to expressing love to someone you know.**

Have each person turn over his or her handout and draw a picture, write a poem, print a word, or tear the paper into a shape that represents a way to show love genuinely to someone. In the meantime, cross out the word "received" on the newsprint you taped to the wall, and write "given" in its place (so the newsprint says, "the greatest gift I've ever given").

Ask teenagers to find their gum shapes on the newsprint and stick their handouts to their shapes. When everyone has finished, have teenagers gather around the sheet and look over the acts of love they've committed to. Close your worship time with a prayer for strength to follow through on the commitments.

Scripture: 1 Corinthians 15:35-58

Theme: The future
Experience: In this **declaration of faith**, teenagers will look to the Bible for encouragement for the future.
Preparation: You'll need a large sheet of paper (at least 2x3 feet), markers, and Bibles.

1 Corinthians

Before the experience, put the large sheet of paper on the floor, and set out markers nearby.

Worship

Give each person a marker. Encourage teenagers to fill the large sheet of paper with future events and possibilities they fear. They may write or draw pictures of such events as graduating from high school, going to war, choosing a college, dying, parents dying, getting a disease, making an irreparable mistake, moving, a friend moving, or being stuck in a boring job.

Then say: **This stuff can be very scary. God knows this. So God has given us specific promises in the Bible to assure us that he will walk with us through these scary things. God has even promised that there is a perfect future waiting for his children after the rough times. Let's worship God and thank him by matching promises from 1 Corinthians 15:35-58 with fears we have.**

Guide teenagers in choosing promises in 1 Corinthians 15:35-58. Help them thank God for the way the promises match the problems they wrote on the piece of paper by writing the promises underneath the problems, along with short prayers of thanks. Have each teenager choose at least one problem and match a promise to it. Here are some examples:

● 1 Corinthians 15:42—"The body that is sown is perishable, it is raised imperishable"—could match "parents dying." A teenager might write this prayer: "Thank you, God, that we'll see each other again, never to be separated. In heaven we'll be safe and together."

● 1 Corinthians 15:55a—"Where, O death, is your victory?"—could match with "going to war." A teenager might write this prayer: "God, even if I have to go to war, eventually you will win the war over death. Then I'll be safe."

● 1 Corinthians 15:50—"I declare to you, brothers, that flesh and blood cannot inherit the kingdom of God, nor does the perishable inherit the imperishable."—could match "not getting into college." A teenager might write this prayer: "Thank you, God, for the message that, no matter what happens, it's the eternal things that matter. Thank you for giving me hope for the future, no matter what direction my life takes."

2 Corinthians

●**Scripture:** 2 Corinthians 4:3-12

Theme: Sharing faith

Experience: In this artistic experience and commissioning, teenagers will discover God's power in their lives and commit to sharing their faith with others.

Preparation: You'll need a Bible, modeling clay, paper, and pens or pencils.

Worship

Read 2 Corinthians 4:3-12 aloud. Ask:

● What does this passage tell us about sharing our faith with others?

Say: In this passage, Paul compares Christians to jars of clay. Ask:

● What do you think Paul means by this comparison?

Say: In Paul's time, people often stored their most valuable possessions in clay jars or pots. They did this because they figured no one would suspect valuable possessions would be kept in the everyday, rather rough-looking clay pots and jars. In the same way, we're simple ordinary humans, but God chose us to carry a priceless treasure within us—his love and his Spirit.

Give each person a fist-sized piece of modeling clay.

Say: I'd like you to take a few moments to create your own clay jar or pot. You can make it any way you'd like. As you create, I'd like you to reflect on the ways you carry God's treasure within you.

Give students a few minutes to create their clay jars, and then give each person a piece of paper and a pen or pencil. Have teenagers form pairs and share their creations with each other, discussing why they chose the form they did and ways they feel they carry God's treasure within them.

Say: Even though we're ordinary, just like these clay jars, we have the tremendous responsibility and privilege to let Christ's light shine through us. I'd like you to think for a moment about specific ways you can let Christ's light shine in your own life. Then write on your piece of paper one action you'll commit to doing in the next week that will demonstrate to others who Jesus is.

Give teenagers a minute to write, and then say:

Now share what you wrote with your partner, and then pray this

2 Corinthians

prayer for each other: God, you've given my partner the power to take your love and light into the world. Please help my partner to show your love during the coming week.

Have teenagers roll or fold their papers and tuck them into their clay jars or pots to take with them.

Scripture: 2 Corinthians 4:13-18

Theme: Faith

Experience: In this **prayer of intercession** and **sharing time**, teenagers will recognize that faith renews their relationship with Jesus.

Preparation: You'll need magazines and newspapers, scissors, glue, poster board, a marker, and Bibles.

Before the experience, cut various pictures and articles from magazines and newspapers that portray the hurt, pain, and sorrow of a sinful world. Use the pictures and articles to make a collage on a piece of poster board. When the collage is complete and the glue is dry, write the word "faith" in large letters across the collage. Then cut the collage into a puzzle that will be challenging for your group to put back together.

Worship

Distribute the puzzle pieces evenly among the students. Then ask:

● What are the stories behind some of your puzzle pieces?

● How have you or your friends experienced this type of pain and hurt?

● What are some ways you or your friends coped with the pain and hurt?

Say: **Now work together to put the puzzle together. When it's complete, we'll talk about it.**

When the puzzle is complete, read 2 Corinthians 4:13-18 aloud and ask:

● How do you feel looking at the collage?

● What does the renewal described in the passage mean to you?

● How do we experience that renewal?

● How can you tell you're being renewed?

● How does your faith play into your renewal process?

● What responsibility do you have in the renewal process?

● How will you experience renewal tomorrow and in the days to come?

After the discussion, gather teenagers around the completed puzzle. Encourage students to pray aloud for the sinful, hurting world the collage represents. Then ask students to pray silently, expressing their faith and asking for God's renewal in their own lives.

End the worship experience by reading 2 Corinthians 4:13-18 aloud together.

2 Corinthians

Scripture: 2 Corinthians 5:20–6:10

Theme: Righteousness

Experience: In this **act of commitment** and **prayer of thanksgiving**, teenagers will celebrate the opportunity to choose the right actions wherever they are.

Preparation: You'll need Bibles.

Worship

Have teenagers form groups of three to five people.

Say: **Because God gives you power, you can choose righteousness—right actions for the right reasons—in any situation. In your group, read 2 Corinthians 5:20–6:10 aloud together.**

Give groups several minutes to read, then have teenagers spread out as much as possible.

Say: **Now I'd like each person to choose one circumstance from the passage and silently tell God two ways you will choose right within that circumstance. Be sure to thank God, too, for giving you the power to follow through on your commitment to do right. For example, you might pray a prayer like this one: God, in *hardships* I will remember that everyone struggles, and I will do my share of sacrificing to make it through. Thanks for your power to help me do this.**

Here are two more examples in case teenagers need more help understanding the worship experience:

God, in *hard work* I will work without complaining, and I will be cheerful in order to cheer up those who work with me. Thanks for your power to help me do this.

God, after *sleepless nights* I will deliberately say the kind word even when I feel like snapping, and I will concentrate hard to keep from going to sleep in school. Thanks for your power to help me do this.

Galatians

Scripture: Galatians 3:23-29

Theme: Unity

Experience: In this **act of praise** and **sharing time**, teenagers will discuss how God has affected them through unity and thank God for making unity possible through Jesus.

Preparation: You'll need Bibles, a candle with a drip catcher for each person, and matches.

Worship

Gather teenagers and say:

> You're all very different from one another, but you can all still be united. In fact, God makes it possible for you to be united with everyone in the world!

Distribute Bibles, and have a volunteer read aloud Galatians 3:23-29 while everyone else reads along.

Say: **Because Jesus died and rose again, everyone in the world has the opportunity to become a son or daughter of God—everyone in the world! If you believe in Jesus, you can be united with everyone else who believes in Jesus.** Ask:

● How would our world be different if Christians lived in unity?

● How would your life be different if you recognized each and every person as a child of God?

● How does our unity influence distinctions between races, classes, and genders?

● How can you change the way you look at others to reflect that you're all united through God's love?

> Say: **Think about a way God has made a difference in your life through unity with others. Create a statement that begins with the words "I thank God for the unity of..." For example, I might say, "I thank God for the unity of my family. We always help each other through tough times."**

As teenagers are thinking, give each student a candle with a drip catcher.

> Say: **Now let's show God our unity by thanking God together for giving us the opportunity to be united through his Son. I'm going to light the first person's candle. That person will tell a second person how God has made a difference in his or her life through unity and**

will light the second person's candle. The second person will tell the third person how God has made a difference in his or her life through unity and will light the third person's candle. Then the third person will tell a fourth person how God has made a difference through unity. We'll continue like this until we're all linked and our candles are lit. Remember that throughout this exercise, we're thanking God.

Light the first person's candle, and turn off the lights. When students are all linked and each person has thanked God, pray:

Dear God, thank you for giving us the opportunity to be united through your Son, and thank you for all that has been accomplished through that unity. Help us love each person as your child so our united love will drive away the darkness just as our candles do. Amen.

Scripture: Galatians 4:4-7

Theme: Sacrifice

Experience: In this **act of commitment** and **offering**, teenagers will commit to sacrifice for others.

Preparation: You'll need a Bible, a photocopy of the "Offering Sheet" handout (p. 56) for each person, pens or pencils, an envelope for each student, and an offering plate or basket.

Worship

Have a few students read Galatians 4:4-7 aloud a verse at a time, then have them discuss the following questions:

● Based on this passage, how do you suppose land, possessions, and other inheritances were passed from one person to another when this passage was written?

  ● What does "full rights of sons" mean in this context?

  ● What does "no longer a slave, but a son" mean in this context?

  ● As an heir, what have you inherited from God?

  ● What did you have to do in order to become an heir?

  ● What did Jesus have to do in order for that inheritance to be given?

Say: We have become heirs to a divine inheritance, even though we don't deserve it. This inheritance is for everybody. Out of our love and thankfulness to our Savior, we extend the same generosity in giving to others as God has given to us, even though they may not deserve it. This is a way God shows his generosity to others—through us, the body of Christ.

Give each person an "Offering Sheet" handout and a pen or pencil, and ask students to fill in their handouts. When students have finished, give

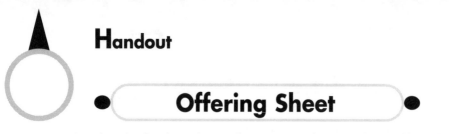

Handout

Offering Sheet

Complete this handout, then seal it in an envelope you have addressed to yourself.

List three ways you can sacrifice each of the following things:

Time

1.

2.

3.

Money

1.

2.

3.

Belongings

1.

2.

3.

List three ways you can make sacrifices for the following people:

Family

1.

2.

3.

Friends

1.

2.

3.

God

1.

2.

3.

them envelopes and ask them to address the envelopes to themselves. Have them put the handouts in envelopes and seal them.

Collect the envelopes in an offering plate or basket, then close in prayer.

Two weeks after the worship experience, mail the envelopes to the students.

Ephesians

Scripture: Ephesians 1:15-23

Theme: Sharing faith

Experience: In this **act of commitment, prayer of petition,** and **prayer of thanskgiving**, teenagers will thank God for the gift of Jesus and commit to sharing the good news.

Preparation: You'll need a paper bag, a snack, a volunteer to visit your class, Bibles, paper, and pens or pencils.

Before the experience, obtain a snack your teenagers will enjoy, and place the snack in a paper bag. Give the bag to a dramatic volunteer who has agreed to visit your room with the prepared bag at the start of class.

Instruct the volunteer to burst into the room just as you begin to speak. Ask him or her to act very excited and seem to have something *wonderful* to share. He or she should say something like, "Oh, here you are! Wait 'til you see this! It's absolutely the coolest thing you could ever have. You're not going to believe it! I just couldn't wait to get here to tell you all about it. You're going to love it!" Have the visitor periodically peek inside the bag as he or she speaks, then leave the bag with you.

Worship

Have teenagers sit in a circle.

Say: **Today we're going to look at a passage from Ephesians. Our topic will be...**

Your visitor should burst into the room with the paper bag, seemingly out of breath and brimming with exciting news. Let the volunteer speak and leave the bag with you.

Ephesians

After the visitor leaves, peek inside the bag yourself.

Say: **Wow! That's right! This is great!**

Then set the bag out of sight.
Teenagers will protest, but say:

Let's get on with our worship.

Have teenagers form small groups, and distribute Bibles to everyone. Have a volunteer from each group read Ephesians 1:15-23 aloud as the rest of the teenagers read along.

Bring out the paper bag. Show teenagers what's inside the bag, then distribute the treat to the teenagers. As teenagers are enjoying the snack, ask:

● **How did you feel when I wouldn't tell you what was in the bag?**

● **What might have happened if Paul had decided not to share the good news about Jesus?**

● **Who told you about Jesus?**

Have teenagers sit in a circle.

Say: **Let's read verses 15 and 16 aloud in unison.**

Read the verse aloud with the young people, then say:

Paul offered prayers of thanks for the faithful people of Ephesus. Think about the person who told you about Jesus. When I say, "Thank you, Lord, for..." say the name of the person who introduced you to Jesus.

Lead the teenagers in the prayer.
Distribute paper and pens or pencils.

Say: **Now think about someone you'd like to tell about Jesus.**

Pause.

In this Bible passage, Paul tells of many of the wonderful qualities of Jesus. Read the passage again, and write down three things Paul said that you'd like to share with the person you thought of.

When teenagers have finished writing, say:

You probably won't use the same language and manner of speech that Paul used. Think of the words you might use to explain the three things you wrote down. Write three sentences that you might actually say—a sort of script you could use. Feel free to consult with one another for advice.

Give teenagers a few minutes to write. Then say:

Just as Paul shared the great news about Jesus in this passage, you can share the great news too. Right now, silently make a commitment to God that you'll use your "script" when the Holy Spirit provides the opportunity.

Pause as teenagers pray.

Now let's close by praying for the people you've thought of. After I say the name of the person I thought of, we'll go around the circle to my left, and you can each say a name. Let's pray. Lord, please open the hearts of the following people to the good news of your Son.

Say the name of your person, then wait as teenagers say names. When everyone has had the opportunity to say a name, close by saying "amen."

Scripture: Ephesians 3:14-21

Theme: Needs

Experience: In this **prayer of intercession**, teenagers will pray for each other's deepest needs.

Preparation: You'll need a Bible, index cards, pens or pencils, and masking tape.

Before the experience, dim the lights in your meeting room.

Worship

Have teenagers form groups of three. Ask each group to come up with a list of basic needs everyone has. Give groups five minutes to think of their lists. When time is up, have groups report their lists of needs to the other groups. When groups have shared, ask:

● What is the deepest need all of us have? Why?

● Is it possible for us to fulfill others' unseen needs, such as healing for emotional struggles or internal bleeding?

● If you believe in Christ, what is your obligation to those who have needs? Explain.

Say: It's interesting that needs can be both seen and unseen. But whether we can see them or not, needs must be met. I'd like you to listen to a passage in the Bible about meeting needs. As I read this to you, I'd like you to identify the need and how it was being met.

Read Ephesians 3:14-19. Ask trios to discuss the following questions:

● What was the need of the people Paul was praying for?

● How did he pray that the need would be met?

Say: Paul gave us some instruction through practical life application. He committed to pray for his friends and their deep needs: for strength, to be rooted and established in love, and to be filled with the fullness of God. All of us have needs. Some needs are deep like the ones Paul prayed for. Today we're going to spend some time in a silent prayer service for one another.

Ask each teenager to find a place alone in the room. Give each person

Ephesians

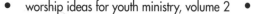

an index card, a pen or pencil, and a piece of masking tape. Have students sit and think about their greatest needs. When each person has thought of his or her greatest need, have that person write the need on the index card and tape it to his or her back.

Then say: **Let's spend some time praying silently for one another. I'd like you to remain completely quiet for the next few minutes. I'd like you to silently walk around the room and find a partner. Once you've found a partner, read the card on his or her back, and silently pray for that need. Then move on to another partner.**

When students have spent several minutes in prayer for one another, close by reading Ephesians 3:20-21 aloud.

Scripture: Ephesians 4:11-16

Theme: The church

Experience: In this **complete service**, teenagers will teach the congregation about the importance of people in the church.

Preparation: You'll need paper, pens or pencils, Bibles, and song books.

Before this experience, arrange for the teenagers to present a twenty- to thirty-minute worship service to the congregation.

Worship

Ask:

● **Do you think you have an important role to play within the church? Explain.**

● **What different roles do you see people carrying out in the church?**

Distribute paper and pens or pencils, and say:

I'm going to read aloud a passage from Ephesians about some of the different roles people fill in the church. As I read, listen for the reasons the church needs people to fill these different roles. When you hear a reason, jot it down on your sheet of paper.

Read aloud Ephesians 4:11-16. Then have teenagers share what they wrote on their sheets of paper. Ask:

● **Why is it important for people in the church to fill different roles?**

● **Why is it important for these people to prepare us for works of service?**

● **How do works of service build up the body of Christ?**

● **How can prophets, evangelists, pastors, and teachers help church members avoid being "tossed back and forth by the waves"?**

Say: **The church, or the body of Christ, is linked together. We all** have jobs to do, and our efforts help others. When we serve one another and build up one another, we can all stand strong and faithful. *Stop.* This is an important message for everyone in the church to hear. We're going to create a worship service that encourages the congregation to recognize Jesus' plan for the church and then respond to it.

When everyone understands the purpose, have teenagers form three groups: the music group, the prayer group, and the message group. Provide Bibles for the message group and song books for the music group, and explain that each group's part of the worship service should last only seven to ten minutes. Encourage the teenagers to be creative as they plan their segments of worship, and remind teenagers of their goal: to help congregation members recognize Jesus' plan for the church and respond to it.

As teenagers work, offer help to all the groups as needed. Continue to encourage teenagers to be creative. For example, suggest to the music group that, instead of simply singing a song, the teenagers lead the congregation in an activity that illustrates how important each person is to the church and praises Jesus for his plan. The activity could have different groups of congregation members drumming different beats with their hands while the teenagers sing a song a cappella that praises Jesus for his plan for the church.

You might suggest to the prayer group that teenagers involve church members in praying to serve one another and to praise God. For example, the congregation could form several groups. Each group could then pray for one of the church's needs. Then the whole congregation could repeat a few lines together to praise Jesus for his plan for the church.

Encourage the message group to use an unusual, involving method to deliver the message. For example, the teenagers could perform a skit that includes volunteers from the congregation. Or they could do a dramatic reading with teenagers positioned throughout the congregation. Remind the message group to teach the Scripture and to lead the congregation to praise Jesus.

After the three groups have finished planning, have them present their ideas to each other. Finally, have them decide in what order to present the worship service to the congregation.

Philippians

Scripture: Philippians 1:3-11

Theme: Encouragement

Experience: In this **act of commitment** and **artistic experience**, teenagers will practice encouraging each other.

Preparation: You'll need Bibles, poster board, scissors, and an assortment of markers.

Before the experience, cut each piece of poster board into four smaller posters. You'll need one poster for each person.

Worship

Have teenagers form pairs. Direct the person who was born first in each pair to read Philippians 1:3-11 aloud to his or her partner, substituting the partner's name for each "you" or "your." For example, Terry's partner would read, "I thank my God every time I remember *Terry*. In all my prayers for *Terry*, I always pray with joy because of *Terry's* partnership in the gospel…"

Then ask the other partner to read in the same manner.

Ask: **As we pray for one another and encourage each other, how do we worship God?**

Give each student a poster, and make markers available to everyone. Direct each person to write his or her name on the poster and copy Philippians 1:3-11.

Say: **Now let's work together as a group to compose a statement that says we'll care for each other, thank God for each other, support each other, and be patient with each other as God completes his work in each of us. Let's put this in our own words, and remember this is a way to worship God.**

When the group has come up with a statement, ask the young people to write this statement around the outside edge of their posters.

Then have teenagers sit in a circle. Ask them to pass the posters to the left so that they can sign the back of each poster as a testimony that they will continue caring for one another as God completes his good work.

Scripture: Philippians 1:21-27

Theme: Living a worthy life

Experience: In this **act of commitment**, teenagers will commit to living lives worthy of the gospel.

Preparation: You'll need Bibles, a chalkboard and chalk or a piece of newsprint and a marker, index cards, and pens or pencils.

Worship

Give each person an index card and a pen or pencil. Have a volunteer read Philippians 1:21-27 aloud. Ask the following questions, and write the group's answers on a chalkboard or a piece of newsprint:

● What are the most extraordinary points of this passage?

● What are some examples of "fruitful labor" in today's times?

● What does "conduct yourselves in a manner worthy of the gospel of Christ" mean?

● What happens when people who identify themselves as Christians fail to "conduct themselves in a manner worthy of the gospel"?

● What are the results when believers "conduct themselves in a manner that is worthy of the gospel"?

Say: For this last question, I'd like each person to come up with one answer, share your answer, and write it on your index card.

Ask: What are specific things this group can do every day that will accurately represent the gospel?

After all the students have answered and recorded their answers on the index cards, have everyone sit in a circle.

Say: We've identified many ways in which we can "conduct ourselves in a manner worthy of the gospel." As Christians, we have a responsibility to present ourselves as people who understand that we were broken and now are made whole by Jesus' death and resurrection. If you want to live a life worthy of the gospel, stand up.

Allow teenagers time to stand, then say:

Let's start living lives worthy of the gospel right now. If you're standing, look at your index card. Then, in the next few minutes, do what you wrote down on your card.

(If some students aren't standing, ask them to sit quietly during this time.)

Some teenagers may not be able to complete the actions they wrote on their cards at that time. Encourage them to formulate plans to do those things later.

Allow teenagers a few minutes to act on what they wrote on their cards. Then gather them back in a circle, and ask them to hold hands.

Say: We'll close our time in prayer by using this format: I'll open our prayer, then we'll go around the circle and identify aloud what we're trying to work on so we can live lives worthy of the gospel. If you aren't willing to commit to doing what your card says, squeeze the hand of the person next to you, and that person will continue. When we've gone around the circle, I'll close our prayer.

Philippians

Scripture: Philippians 2:1-11

Theme: Humility

Experience: In this **artistic experience** and **prayer of intercession,** teenagers will compare exalting themselves and humbling themselves; then they'll pray for each other.

Preparation: You'll need newsprint, scissors, tape, colorful markers, and Bibles.

Before the experience, tape a small square—about 2x2 feet—of newsprint on the floor. Cut a second square of newsprint the same size for use later.

Worship

Say: **It's fun to brag about yourself sometimes, isn't it? When you work hard and do a good job, you want people to know. That's only natural. I've taped a piece of newsprint to the floor, and I want you all to gather around that newsprint and draw something you're really proud of yourself for.**

Show teenagers the piece of newsprint, make markers available to them all, and encourage them to jump in and draw what they're proud of. After a few minutes, tell teenagers time is up. Then ask:

● **What was it like to draw something you're proud of?**
● **Was it easy or difficult to draw on this piece of paper? Explain.**
● **What was it like to draw when everyone else was drawing? Explain.**

Say: **It's OK to be enthusiastic about something you've accomplished. But just as you all had to share the paper, the markers, and the drawing space to draw your accomplishments, we all need to make sure our pride doesn't get in the way of caring for others.**

Distribute Bibles, and then say:

Take a couple of minutes to read Philippians 2:1-11 to yourself. Really think about what God is saying to you through the words. Really think about the example Jesus set for us.

As teenagers are reading, tape another small square of newsprint to the floor. After a couple of minutes, ask:

● **What does Jesus' example teach us?**
● **Why is humility so important?**
● **How can your life reflect Christ's humility?**

Say: **I've taped another piece of newsprint to the floor. This time, I want each of you to draw a picture to show God an example of humility as described in the Scripture you just read. Through your drawing, show God what you understand humility to be. While you draw,** continue to think about Christ's example and how your life can reflect his humility.

Encourage teenagers to gather around the newsprint again. After a few minutes of drawing, ask:

● What was it like to share the newsprint, markers, and drawing space?

● Did focusing on Christ's example of humility change what you drew or how you interacted with others as you drew? Explain.

● What difference can humility make in your life outside this room?

Have teenagers form a circle around the pictures of humility.

Say: **Now as an example to God of humility, let's look to the interests of others by silently praying for one another to achieve humility.**

After a minute or two of prayer, close by saying:

Dear God, thank you so much for Jesus' example of humility. Help us to humble ourselves as Jesus did. In Jesus' name, amen.

Colossians

Scripture: Colossians 1:15-29

Theme: Salvation

Experience: In this **act of praise**, teenagers will build paper bridges to affirm that Jesus is our bridge to God.

Preparation: You'll need Bibles, markers, and paper.

Worship

Have teenagers form pairs, and give each pair a Bible. In their pairs, have teenagers read Colossians 1:15-29.

When teenagers have finished reading, say:

In your pairs, discuss these questions. Be prepared to share your answers with the rest of the group. Ask:

● According to this passage, what prevents us from getting to God?

● What does this passage say is the only way to God?

Say: **The Bible says we're reconciled to God only through Jesus. Once people were separated from God because of their sin. But because of Jesus and what he did on the cross, we have a way back to God and eternal life with him. Jesus is our bridge.**

Have pairs move to one side of the room. Give each pair a marker and a supply of paper. Place a Bible on a table on the other side of the room.

Say: **Let's say this Bible represents God. Since Jesus is our bridge, we'll choose attributes of Jesus mentioned in the passage we read to build bridges to the Bible. On each piece of paper, write one attribute of Jesus mentioned in the passage. One partner will write on the paper, then place the paper on the floor for the other partner to walk on. Halfway across the room, partners will switch roles. Ready?**

When all pairs have reached the Bible, have teenagers sit in a circle. Collect the papers from the floor.

Say: **As an act of praise and worship, let's read these attributes of Jesus. I'll pass the pile of papers around to my left. When the papers come to you, read aloud what's written on the top paper, then offer a silent prayer of thanksgiving to Jesus for that quality. Keep the paper and pass the rest on. When we've finished, you should have several papers to take home to remind you of Jesus' wonderful qualities.**

①Thessalonians

Scripture: 1 Thessalonians 4:13-14

Theme: Hope

Experience: In this creative writing experience, teenagers will express their hope in Christ.

Preparation: You'll need a Bible, pens or pencils, and a "Letter to God" handout (p. 68) for each person.

Worship

Have a student read 1 Thessalonians 4:13-14 aloud. Then ask:

What does "those who have fallen asleep" refer to?

Say: Paul wrote this text in a letter to the Thessalonian church about those who had died. He did this because the people of the church were very concerned about the salvation of their friends who were Christians and had died prior to Jesus' return. Paul reminded them of the hope they shared in the fact that Jesus had already proved he was God by his resurrection. Paul assured the Christians that their friends were sure to be resurrected and meet Jesus.

● Where was Paul, the writer, saying they could get their hope?
● How do we know that we can have hope in these matters?
● What are the differences between faith and hope?
● How does Jesus' resurrection give you hope?

Give each person a "Letter to God" handout and say:

Use this handout as a skeleton for a letter you'll write to God. You have several minutes, so take your time and communicate carefully what you would like to say to God.

Scripture: 1 Thessalonians 5:1-11

Theme: Jesus' return

Experience: In this **artistic experience** and **meditation**, teenagers will create visual representations of ways to prepare for Jesus' return.

Preparation: You'll need newspaper; Bibles; craft supplies such as newsprint, markers, glue, tape, felt, paint, and craft sticks; index cards; and pens or pencils. Before the experience, cover a table with newspaper, and set the craft supplies on the table.

Worship

Read 1 Thessalonians 5:1-11 aloud, and ask:

What are some ways we can prepare for Jesus' return?

Have teenagers form three groups, and give each group a Bible. Assign verses 1-3 to one group, verses 4-7 to the second group, and verses 8-11 to the third group.

Say: I'd like you to read through your assigned verses and think of a way you might represent the theme of your verses. Then I'd like you to use the craft supplies on this table to create something that represents the theme. You'll have about ten minutes to do this.

A Letter to God

Those who believe that Jesus died on the cross and was raised from the dead to pay for humanity's rebellion against God have hope. They've been forgiven for all the wrong things they've done because Jesus already paid the penalty for those sins. As a result, they have hope for eternal life with God in a way that is unimaginable. They can have hope, too, that others who have passed away will also be resurrected someday at God's discretion. Fill out the following work sheet as if you were talking to God.

Dear God,

My name is _____, and I feel
                               (your name)
_____ when I think about what you've done for me.
   (feeling word)

You are _____, _____, and _____. I don't al-
        (adjective)   (adjective)   (adjective)
ways understand you or my relationship with you, but I do hope for

_____, _____, and _____. I hope for these
  (noun)   (noun)   (noun)
things because I know that you _____, _____, and
                             (verb)   (verb)
_____ for me.
  (verb)

Please allow me to _____ so I may _____ in the future.
              (verb)   (verb)

Love,

_____
   (your name)

Word Key

Adjective = describing word (such as wonderful, big, or beautiful)
Noun = person, place, or thing (such as love, house, or mom)
Verb = action word (such as sing, run, or stop)

When you're finished, choose a representative to present your group's creation to the rest of us.

Give teenagers ten minutes, then have them share their creations in order of their assigned verses. Then say:

As this passage tells us, we have no idea when Jesus will return. No matter how hard we try to figure it out, only God knows the time. Until Jesus returns, we should prepare our hearts and minds for that day.

Give each person an index card and a pen or pencil.

Say: I'd like you to think of one thing that you feel God might be saying to you personally in this passage. Reflect on what really stood out for you as we read this passage and created visual representations.

Give teenagers several minutes to reflect and write. Then say:

I'd like you to take your card with you and put it in a place where you'll see it regularly, perhaps in your locker or on a bathroom mirror. When you see it, reflect on things you can do right now to prepare for Jesus' return.

2 Thessalonians

Scripture: 2 Thessalonians 1:1-12

Theme: Prayer

Experience: In this **prayer of intercession**, teenagers will pray for people who are suffering.

Preparation: You'll need newsprint, markers, masking tape, Bibles, a CD or cassette of soft music, and a CD or cassette player.

Before the experience, write "people who are suffering" on a sheet of newsprint. Write "people who need endurance" on another sheet. Tape the two sheets of newsprint to a wall in your meeting area.

2 Thessalonians

Worship

Have teenagers form groups of three or four and read 2 Thessalonians 1:1-10 in their groups. Ask:

● When have you suffered? Explain.

● What's the worst suffering you've ever heard of?

● How did the person handle it?

● Does knowing that God will help you when you suffer ease the pain of suffering? Explain.

Say: **Suffering is tough. God wants us to understand that he knows when we're suffering. And when we hurt, God hurts. When we suffer, God suffers with us. I'd like you to identify people you know who either are suffering or need endurance.**

Have groups go to each sheet of newsprint and read the topic. Then ask them to write on the newsprint descriptions of people who are suffering or situations in which people need endurance to make it through difficult situations.

When groups have finished writing, say:

This passage doesn't just leave us with the knowledge that people suffer or need endurance. It offers the promise that if we'll lift these situations up in prayer, God will hear.

Read 2 Thessalonians 1:11-12.

Say: **Knowing that someone needs prayer really doesn't solve the problem. What's most important is that when we know someone is suffering, we pray for that person. So let's go back through these situations and lift up these concerns to God.**

Play some soft music while groups go to each sheet of newsprint and pray silently for the needs described there. Encourage groups to pray for all the requests on the newsprint, not just theirs.

1 Timothy

Scripture: 1 Timothy 2:1-4

Theme: Praying for leaders

Experience: In this **prayer of intercession**, teenagers will identify those in authority and pray specifically for them as directed by Scripture.

Preparation: You'll need newsprint and a marker or a chalkboard and chalk, a Bible, candles, matches, a CD or cassette of soft music, and a CD or cassette player.

Worship

Say: **In 1 Timothy 2, Paul gives us instructions on how to worship God. He begins by saying that we should pray for everyone, particularly for people in authority. Today we're going to identify those in authority and pray specifically for them.**

Remind youth that authority means the power or right to make final decisions, give commands, take action, create laws, and enforce obedience. Have teenagers identify those in authority in the nation, the state or province, the city, their schools, the church, and their families. List the names on newsprint or a chalkboard so everyone can see them.

Read 1 Timothy 2:1-4 aloud. Ask:

● **Why should we obey those in authority in our lives?**

● **What are some specific prayers you would offer to God for some of the people we listed?**

Say: **Now let's spend some time praying for these people. As we prepare to pray, silently ask the Holy Spirit to direct our prayers.**

Light some candles, and play some soft music.

Begin by slowly reading 1 Timothy 2:1-4 aloud. Then read the names of the listed authority figures one by one, allowing time after each name for teenagers to pray specifically for that person.

Read as many names as you have time for. Close with a group prayer, asking God to help guide those in authority.

1 Timothy

Scripture: 1 Timothy 6:6-16

Theme: Putting God first

Experience: In this **act of commitment**, teenagers will commit to keeping God first in their lives.

Preparation: You'll need Bibles.

Worship

Have teenagers form three groups. Have groups read 1 Timothy 6:6-16. When they've finished, say:

> Many of us struggle with loving money more than we love God. If we're not careful, the desire to get rich can consume us. But wanting to get rich isn't the only thing we struggle with. Actually, we can struggle with allowing *anything* to get in the way of our relationship with God.

Have each group create a two-minute skit about something a person might put ahead of God. After teenagers have had a few minutes to prepare, have groups present their skits. Then ask:

● Why do we tend to put these things ahead of God?

● How can we overcome the temptation to put things ahead of God?

● What is a person's life like when that person puts God ahead of everything else?

Say: **Now I'd like each group to offer advice to another group. Give that group some ideas about how to overcome the specific struggle presented in the group's skit.**

Encourage groups to share their advice with each other.

Then gather teenagers in the center of your meeting area, and say:

> I'm going to ask you to make a serious commitment. I'd like you to commit to putting God ahead of every desire, action, and thought for the next week. If you don't feel you're ready to make this commitment, spend the time praying for the people who are committing to keeping God first.
>
> If you're ready to make this commitment, I'd like you to stand and respond by saying "I will" after each statement I read.

Read the following statements, and allow time for teenagers to respond to each one:

● Will you flee from the desire to put unimportant things ahead of God?

● Will you pursue righteousness, faith, and love?

● Will you seek endurance and gentleness?

● Will you try to see others the way God sees them?

● Will you keep God first in all you say and do?

Close your commitment time with a short prayer.

2 Timothy

Scripture: 2 Timothy 2:8-13

Theme: Serving Christ

Experience: In this **prayer of confession**, teenagers will recognize the struggles they face in trying to serve Christ.

Preparation: You'll need construction paper, scissors, a Bible, a chalkboard and chalk or newsprint and a marker, markers, and tape.

Before the experience, write these two headings at the top of a chalkboard or a piece of newsprint: "serving Christ" and "stumbling blocks." Cut strips of construction paper (about one inch wide and five inches long). You'll need seven paper strips for each person.

Worship

Read 2 Timothy 2:8-13 aloud.

Say: **I'm going to reread this Scripture passage. I'd like you to call out words or phrases that describe a life that's totally devoted to serving Christ.**

Then begin rereading each sentence slowly.

As teenagers call out words and phrases, write them on the chalkboard or newsprint under the "serving Christ" heading. If teenagers need help, suggest such phrases as "Remember Jesus Christ," "endure everything," and "died with him."

When the list is complete, say:

Now let's list some things that can act as stumbling blocks to serving Christ—cheating on exams, lying to parents, or breaking trust with friends, for example.

As teenagers call out ideas, write them on the chalkboard or newsprint under the "stumbling blocks" heading.

Give each person seven construction paper strips, and make markers and tape available to everyone.

Say: **On each paper strip, write one stumbling block you struggle with in serving Christ.**

When teenagers have written on their paper strips, show them how to create paper chains: Tape the ends of one paper strip together so it forms a circle. Put the end of another paper strip through that circle, and tape the

2 Timothy

ends of that paper strip together so the two circles are linked. Continue this process until the paper strips form a seven-link chain.

Say: **It's important to recognize these stumbling blocks so we can avoid them with God's help. Sin weighs us down and keeps us chained up. Serving Christ sets us free and gives us joy. Let's participate together in a prayer of confession, admitting these struggles to God and asking for God's help in overcoming them.**

Have youth form a circle.

Say: **I'll begin a prayer of confession, and I'd like you to participate with me. We'll confess to God that we don't always serve Christ in the ways we listed earlier.**

Point out the "serving Christ" list on the chalkboard or newsprint.

Pray aloud: **Dear God, we confess that we so often fail to serve you the way we should and the way we want to. Please forgive us when we fail to...**

Encourage teenagers to participate with you in reading the expectations on the "serving Christ" list.

Then say: **Now we'll confess to God that we are sometimes tripped by the stumbling blocks in our way. After I begin our prayer of confession, I'd like you to spend some time in silent prayer, reading the things you wrote on your paper chains and admitting them one at a time to God.**

Pray: **God, we also want to confess the wrong things we've done. Please help us as we struggle with the stumbling blocks that keep us away from you. Help us not to give in to these struggles...**

Pause for a few minutes, allowing teenagers to spend time in silent confession.

After the prayer time, encourage youth to take their chains home with them and remove one link each day, saying a prayer for specific help in overcoming that stumbling block.

Scripture: 2 Timothy 3:14–4:5

Theme: The Bible

Experience: In this **prayer of intercession** and **sharing time**, teenagers will write prayers for each other, asking for God's guidance in studying the Bible.

Preparation: You'll need Bibles, paper, and pens or pencils.

Worship

Say: **The Apostle Paul had sort of a mentoring relationship with a**

2 Timothy

young man named Timothy. He wrote to Timothy, encouraging him to use his gift of teaching to help others. Paul was in prison, and he didn't even know how much longer he'd be alive. So he wrote very important, urgent, and inspiring words to Timothy.

Have teenagers open their Bibles and turn to 2 Timothy 3:14–4:5.

Say: **As we read this Scripture, remember that the Bible is God's Word. Hear these words as if God were saying them specifically to you.**

Have several volunteers read the passage aloud, a verse at a time, as everyone else reads along silently. Then say:

Now find a partner, and talk with your partner about what you would like to say to God, or even ask God, in response to this Scripture.

After a minute or two of discussion, ask partners to share ways God has made a difference in their lives through his Word. After some discussion, say:

Now talk with each other about obstacles that discourage you from reading the Bible.

After some discussion, say:

Now talk with each other about how God can help you overcome those obstacles.

Distribute paper and pens or pencils, and say:

Now turn your back to your partner. Think again about God's words in the Scripture we read, and think about your discussion with your partner. Then write a prayer for your partner. First praise God for his Word, thanking God for specific ways the Bible has made a difference in your partner's life. Then ask God to help your partner with the obstacles that discourage him or her from studying the Bible. Address not only the specific obstacles you discussed, but also your partner's response to the Scripture. Finally ask God for specific kinds of help based on your discussion with your partner. For example, maybe your partner needs help organizing time or needs a motivating friend to study the Bible with.

Give teenagers several minutes to think and write their prayers. Remind teenagers to be specific in their prayers and to thank God as well as ask for help. Then say:

Now turn back toward your partner. Take a minute to pray together by reading the prayer you wrote.

After the teenagers have finished their prayers, encourage them to take their written prayers home and continue praying regularly for their partners.

Titus

Scripture: Titus 2:11–3:7

Theme: Salvation

Experience: In this **creative writing experience** and **sharing time**, teenagers will celebrate the effect that knowing Jesus has had on their lives.

Preparation: You'll need newsprint, markers, tape, Bibles, paper, and pens or pencils.

Before the experience, tape a sheet of newsprint to a wall in your meeting area. Divide the newsprint down the middle. At the top of one side, write "before" and on the other side write "after."

Worship

Gather teenagers together and say:

> **Have you ever thought of the difference between what you were like before you knew Jesus and what you're like now? I'd like to read you a passage about some people who were greatly changed as a result of their relationships with Jesus.**

Read Titus 2:11–3:7.

Say: **This passage is about two very different kinds of life—life before knowing Christ and life after knowing him. I'd like you to look for some of those differences in the passage.**

Have teenagers form two groups, and make sure each group has a Bible. Ask one group to look for descriptions of life before knowing Christ and the other to look for descriptions of life after knowing Christ. Direct groups to record their findings on the sheet of newsprint taped to the wall.

When groups have finished, say:

> **The differences in a person's life before and after that person knows Christ can be amazing. Even though all those lifestyle changes don't usually happen at once, Jesus does change us from what we used to be into new creations.**

Have the teenagers sit by themselves. Give each person paper and a pen or pencil, then ask the students to write short stories that describe their lives before and after they became Christians. When teenagers have finished writing, have them form groups of three or four and share their stories.

Close the worship time with a short prayer, thanking God for making people into new creations.

Philemon

Scripture: Philemon 4-21

Theme: Forgiveness

Experience: In this **meditation**, teenagers will reflect on God's forgiveness and how they can pass forgiveness on to others.

Preparation: You'll need Bibles, paper, pens or pencils, and a small trash can or basket.

Worship

Have teenagers form a circle. Let students take turns reading the verses from Philemon 4-21.

Say: **Onesimus (oh-NES-ih-mus) was a slave who Paul sent back to his wealthy master, Philemon (fih-LEE-mun). We can tell from this passage that Paul wanted Philemon to forgive Onesimus and welcome him just as he would have welcomed Paul. But the Bible doesn't really tell us the outcome of the story.**

Ask: **What do you think happened to Onesimus when he returned to Philemon?**

Say: **In this passage, Paul was willing to pay any debt that Onesimus had incurred.**

Ask: **How is that like the way Jesus paid the debt for our sins?**

Give each person two pieces of paper and a pen or pencil.

Say: **Think of one particular sin you've committed that you're glad Jesus has erased from your record. Write that sin on one of your pieces of paper.**

Give the teenagers time to think and write.

The Bible says that when God forgives us, it's as though we never committed a sin. I'm going to pass around this trash can. When it comes to you, silently thank God for forgiving your sin, then tear your paper in half and throw away your "sin." Then pass the trash can on.

After the basket has been returned to you, say:

It's wonderful knowing that God forgives and forgets our sins.

Ask: **What would it be like if God were to pull that forgiven sin out continually and hold it against you again and again?**

Hebrews

Say: **Now think of one person you need to forgive. Write the person's name on your other piece of paper, then write one word that represents what you need to forgive that person for.**

Give teenagers a few moments to reflect and write.

Say: **It was pretty easy to throw away our "sins" and accept God's forgiveness, wasn't it? But it's a lot harder to forgive someone else in the same complete way. Think about whether you're really ready to forgive the person you wrote about. Remember, once you forgive that person, you can never pull that sin out and bring it up again. Say a silent prayer, asking God to help you forgive that person as completely as God forgives you.**

Pause as teenagers pray.

Say: **I'm going to pass around this trash can again. If you're ready to truly forgive the person whose name you wrote, tear your paper in half and put the pieces in the trash can. Remember, you must be willing to throw away any resentment or anger forever, just as God does in forgiving you. If you're not quite able to forgive in that way yet, keep your paper and pass the trash can on. Continue to ask God during week to help you forgive. We'll all keep our heads down as the trash can is passed, because this issue is strictly between you and God.**

When the trash can comes back to you, close with a prayer thanking God for his love and forgiveness and asking him to help us forgive others in the same way.

Hebrews

Scripture: Hebrews 4:1-13

Theme: Salvation

Experience: In this **meditation,** teenagers will experience the joy that comes from receiving God's grace.

Preparation: You'll need Bibles, a photocopy of the "Hebrews 4:1-13 Bible Study" (p. 80) handout for each person, and pens or pencils. This worship experience works best if done at the end of a long, strenuous activity, such as hiking, backpacking, or camping.

Worship

After a long day of hiking, backpacking, camping, or other strenuous activity, gather teenagers and say:

We're all tired and in need of rest. We're going to spend some time in independent, quiet Bible study. It should take you between ten minutes and an hour to complete the Bible study. Find a quiet place with as little distraction as possible, and follow the directions of the guided study. When you've completed the study, please remain quiet out of respect for those who are still participating in the study.

Give each person a "Hebrews 4:1-13 Bible Study" handout, a Bible, and a pen or pencil and make yourself available for questions.

Scripture: Hebrews 4:14-16

Theme: Jesus understands

Experience: In this **sharing time**, teenagers will affirm that Jesus sympathizes with their struggles.

Preparation: You'll need Bibles and a photocopy of the "Sympathy Exercise" handout (p. 82) for each student.

Worship

Give each person a "Sympathy Exercise" handout.

Say: This exercise may make some people feel uncomfortable because it requires some sharing. If at any time you don't feel comfortable sharing with another person, you have the right to say, "I don't want to talk about it."

The purpose of the handout I've given you is to help you sympathize with other people who have had some of the same experiences you've had. Read through your handout until you find a situation you've experienced. Then find someone else in the room who has experienced the same thing. When you find a person who shares your experience, talk with that person about the experience. We'll do this for about ten minutes.

If necessary, allow teenagers to form some groups of three to discuss their shared experiences. After approximately ten minutes, ask:

● What was it like to talk about your experiences with someone who has had the same experiences?

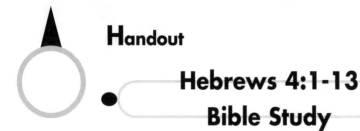

Handout

Hebrews 4:1-13
Bible Study

Follow these steps as you use this time to grow in your faith.

1. Begin your time with a prayer of thanksgiving.

   What are you thankful for?

   Who are you thankful for?

   Why are you thankful?

2. Write your answers to the following questions.

   Describe what you did today.

   What are three words that would describe how you're feeling physically?

   What are three words that would describe how you're feeling emotionally?

   What are three words that would describe how you're feeling spiritually?

3. Read Hebrews 4:1-13.

4. Write your answers to the following questions.

   What does it mean to fall short of God's rest?

   What does it mean to enter God's rest?

   What work are we supposed to rest from?

   How have you tried to gain God's favor by the work you do?

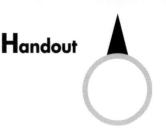

5. Read the information below.

> This passage uses rest as a metaphor for accepting Christ's salvation—resting from things we do to try to gain God's favor. Many times, Christians forget why they're doing things "for God" in the first place.
>
> Sometimes we think that God will love us and accept us only if we're doing all kinds of things to make God happy. That isn't the case. We can do nothing to make God love us and accept us more than he already does. Our motivation for doing something "for God" should come from our thankfulness for the grace God has given us. That grace gives us the joy of knowing that God is active in our lives and that we'll spend eternity with God.
>
> Nothing we do can ever make God love us more. Jesus Christ has given us spiritual rest.

6. Answer these questions.

> How does that make you feel?
>
> Can you accept the fact that Jesus loves you no matter what? What might make that acceptance a struggle for you?
>
> What are three words that come to your mind, knowing that your rest comes in your salvation?

7. As you close your time here, take a few minutes to praise the Lord for the spiritual rest God has given you. Look at the sets of words that you used to describe how you felt physically, emotionally, and spiritually. Pray that God will lead you to opportunities to rest in those areas so you may become a more effective disciple of Jesus.

Sympathy Exercise

Read the situations below, and find one that you've experienced. Then find another person who has experienced the same one. Take some time to share your story and hear the story of the other person.

Have you ever experienced...

- breaking a bone in your body?

- getting stitches?

- being in a car accident?

- sitting on a big wad of freshly chewed gum?

- the divorce of your parents?

- the death of somebody close to you?

- a really embarrassing moment in a public place?

- a bloody nose?

- public speaking?

- motion sickness from an amusement park ride?

● How might this shared experience affect your relationship with the person you were sharing with?

Ask a volunteer to read Hebrews 4:14-16 aloud. Then ask:

● When this passage was written, what role did the high priest have in the community? What significance did he have to that culture?

● How does Jesus fill the role of high priest to those who follow him?

● How is Jesus able to sympathize with our weaknesses?

● What role do shared experiences play in trusting relationships?

● What experiences have you had that Jesus might have shared?

● How might these shared experiences affect your relationship with Jesus?

Have students form a circle and join hands.

Say: **In our lives here on earth, we experience darkness, loneliness, pain, and despair. Jesus has already experienced and conquered all those struggles. He knows us, as our God and as our friend. Now please take a minute of silence to consider the struggle you've been dwelling on.**

Give students one minute to consider their struggles. Then say: **Jesus has been tempted in every way. He knows how you're feeling, what you're thinking, and where you're going. He experienced all these things so he could die for us and wash our sins away forever. If you feel comfortable sharing, tell the rest of the group a short story about how Jesus has helped you through a difficult time.**

Allow teenagers several minutes to share their stories. You may want to share your own story as well. After everyone has had a chance to share, pray aloud, thanking Jesus for understanding us.

Scripture: Hebrews 9:11-28

Theme: Salvation

Experience: In this celebration of the Lord's Supper, teenagers will remember that Jesus' death made it possible for everyone to have a relationship with God.

Preparation: You'll need masking tape, small colored stickers and one sticker that's different, Bibles, snacks, a bag of candy bars, newsprint, markers, and elements for the Lord's Supper

Before the experience, use masking tape to divide your meeting room into three sections. Label each section with one of the following: "All may enter," "Chosen may enter," "Do not enter." If necessary, arrange for a member of the clergy to serve the Lord's Supper to the group at the appropriate time.

Hebrews

Worship

As teenagers arrive, place a small sticker on about half the students. Place a special sticker on one student. Instruct students to gather in the area labeled "All may enter."

When everyone has arrived, say:

I'd like to invite those of you with stickers to enter the "Chosen may enter" area and have a snack. If you aren't one of the chosen, please stay where you are.

Invite teenagers with stickers into the chosen area, and give them their snacks. Then ask:

● How does it feel knowing you aren't one of the chosen?
● How does it feel being one of the chosen?

Then say:

One of you has been selected as a special, chosen person.

Find the person with the special sticker, and say:

Not only can you have access to snacks, you can also have your own bag of candy bars.

Have that person take the snack into the "Do not enter" area, and give him or her the bag of candy bars. Ask:

● How does it feel to be the special, chosen person?
● How do the rest of you feel about this?

Say: **You're looking at a representation of the way things were before Jesus came to earth and died for our sins. Before Jesus came, the only access people had to God was through special priests who took other people's offerings into the Most Holy Place in the tabernacle. But since Christ's death, this isn't the way things are at all.**

Gather everyone in the center of your meeting room, and give everyone snacks and candy bars.

Say: **This is exactly what Jesus' death did. It made it possible for us to have a real, personal relationship with God.**

Have teenagers form groups of three, and give each group a piece of newsprint and a marker, and a Bible. Ask groups to read Hebrews 9:11-28. As teenagers read through the passage, have them list the differences between Jesus and the Old Testament priest. After they've made their lists, have groups report the differences they noticed. Ask:

● What's the difference between the Old Testament tabernacle and our churches?

● What's the difference between the Old Testament people's relationship with God and our relationship with him today?

Say: Jesus paid the price for our sins. Without him we would have no hope. But because he loves us—and gave his life in our place—we can be forgiven of our sins and live forever with God.

Participate in the Lord's Supper with your group. Then close the meeting with a short prayer, thanking Jesus for his death on our behalf.

Scripture: Hebrews 10:19-39

Theme: Faith

Experience: In this **meditation** and **sharing time**, teenagers will encourage each other to choose faith.

Preparation: You'll need Bibles, pens or pencils, and a photocopy of the "Hebrews 10:19-39 Study" handout (p. 86-87) for each person.

Worship

Have teenagers form groups of four, and ask group members to sit close together, with just enough space to fit their knees in the middle. The idea is to give a feeling of togetherness without invading personal space. Be sure each person has a Bible. Ask groups to read Hebrews 10:19-39 aloud.

Give each student a pen or pencil and a copy of the "Hebrews 10:19-39 Study" handout.

Say: Faith is a choice. Daily, with each word and attitude, we can choose or deny God. As you listen to one another's insights about Hebrews 10:19-39, understand one another and remind one another that you believe in everyone's ability to choose faith.

Direct teenagers to read their handouts, refer to the matching Bible passage in their Bibles, and mark their own answers to each question.

When students have finished working through their handouts, ask teenagers to share their answers to the first question within their groups and tell why they answered as they did. Do the same for the rest of the questions on the handout. Encourage youth to take plenty of time to hear and understand one another. Let it be a time of worshipful sharing.

When groups have finished their discussions, ask:

● What have you discovered about deliberately choosing faith?
● Why is faith a daily choice?
● How will you choose to live by Hebrews 10:24-25?

Scripture: Hebrews 11:1-18

Theme: Faith

Experience: In this **creative reading**, teenagers will commemorate the stories of four faith heroes of the Bible.

Hebrews 10:19-39
Study

1. Hebrews 10:19-22 is full of Old Testament sacrificial language. My favorite message in these verses is…
  a. The Most Holy Place is the place nearest God. Because of Jesus, we can come near to God any time and any place.
  b. In the Old Testament worship system, the priests cleansed themselves with water to symbolize cleansing guilt. With God's forgiveness, I'm cleansed of my guilt. God knows what I've done, but because Jesus has already paid for my sin, God looks past that to love me fully and completely.
  c. Nobody is good enough for God. But we can approach God confidently and sincerely because God has come to us in Jesus.
  d. Confidence comes from God, not from anything we do or don't do.

2. It's easy to be faithful to God when everyone around me is being faithful. The times I swerve from God, as warned against in Hebrews 10:23, are…
  a. when I'm tired or grouchy.
  b. when I'm trying to impress someone.
  c. when I fear faithfulness to God will cost me.
  d. when a specific sin seems particularly appealing.

3. I like being spurred on toward love and good deeds by other Christians (Hebrews 10:24-25). My favorite way to give/receive encouragement is…
  a. to give/receive an encouraging smile that only that person sees.
  b. to give/receive a word that communicates, "You can do it."
  c. to demonstrate an attitude that communicates, "I'm with you all the way."
  d. to stand up for someone/be stood up for.

4. Although I know how dreadful it is to ignore or betray God as described in Hebrews 10:26-31, I do it when…
  a. I take God too lightly by _____.
  b. I make the excuse that "God will understand just this once."
  c. I underestimate the incredible sacrifice Jesus made when he gave himself for me.
  d. I'm afraid of what other people will think.

5. As Hebrews 10:32-34 says, I'm reminded to choose the right thing by the early-in-my-faith experience of...
  a. standing my ground on _____.
  b. suffering successfully through _____.
  c. standing by someone who was publicly hurt by

  _____.

  d. focusing on possessions that are lasting rather than material. My favorite nonmaterial possession is _____.

6. Because of the truths in Hebrews 10:35-39, I will refuse to "shrink back" no matter what pressures I feel. I will do this by...
  a. remembering God's rich rewards, including._____.

  b. looking forward to what God has promised. My favorite promise is

  _____.

  c. remembering that the only good life is the one God approves ("my righteous one will live by faith").

  d. recognizing that shrinking back isn't worth it.

Hebrews

Preparation: You'll need a photocopy of the "By Faith We Believe" creative reading (p. 89-90) for each person.

Worship

Ask:

● What is faith?

● What are some examples of Christian beliefs that are based on faith?

Say: Hebrews 11:1 says, "Faith is being sure of what we hope for and certain of what we do not see," and the dictionary defines faith as "unquestioning belief that does not require proof or evidence." Today we're going to express our own faith in God by remembering what faith meant in the lives of four Bible characters.

Give each person a copy of the "By Faith We Believe" creative reading. Assign the eight narrator parts and the four reader parts. If you have fewer than twelve students, assign more than one narrator part to each narrator. If you have more than twelve students, have the remaining teenagers act out the stories of Abel, Enoch, Noah, and Abraham at the appropriate times in the creative reading. You may want to have these teenagers form four groups and have each group act out the part of a different character. Give everyone about five minutes to read through the script, then have youth perform the creative reading.

Scripture: Hebrews 12:1-13

Theme: Endurance

Experience: In this creative reading, teenagers will compare Christian living to running a race.

Preparation: You'll need a Bible and a photocopy of "The Runner: A Creative Reading" handout (p. 91) for each person.

Worship

Ask teenagers to sit on the floor, bow their heads, and close their eyes. Lead a prayer committing to follow Jesus above all other pursuits and desires. Then, while teenagers still have their eyes closed, read Hebrews 12:1-13 aloud to the group.

Say: Think about the image used in this passage. What comes to mind as you hear the writer of Hebrews challenge his readers to "run with perseverance the race marked out for us"? Can you picture a long-distance runner sweating and pouring out every ounce of energy to maintain the grueling pace? Imagine the depth of concentration required to force an exhausted body to keep going. Step

By Faith
We Believe

(based on Hebrews 11:1-18)

Narrator 1: "Now faith is being sure of what we hope for and certain of what we do not see. This is what the ancients were commended for. By faith we understand that the universe was formed at God's command, so that what is seen was not made out of what was visible" *(Hebrews 11:1-3)*.

Reader 1: My name is Abel. My parents were Adam and Eve, and I had an older brother named Cain. I was a shepherd who tended flocks, and Cain was a farmer who worked the soil. When it came time to harvest his crops, my brother offered some of the fruits of the soil to the Lord. I also made an offering to the Lord from the firstborn of my flock of sheep. The Lord was pleased with my offering, but not with Cain's, and he told Cain that he must master the sin that was "crouching at his door." One day Cain asked me to go out to the field with him, and then he killed me. The Lord cursed my brother, and he became a restless wanderer on the earth.

Narrator 2: "By faith Abel offered God a better sacrifice than Cain did. By faith he was commended as a righteous man, when God spoke well of his offerings. And by faith he still speaks, even though he is dead" *(Hebrews 11:4)*.

Reader 2: My name is Enoch. I'm the son of Jared, a descendant of Seth, who was Adam and Eve's third son. My father lived for 962 years. I walked with God for 365 years, and I had many sons and daughters, including my son Methuselah. You may have heard of him; he lived 969 years. I tried to serve God all my life, and in the end God just took me away.

Narrator 3: "By faith Enoch was taken from this life, so that he did not experience death; he could not be found, because God had taken him away. For before he was taken, he was commended as one who pleased God. And without faith it is impossible to please God, because anyone who comes to him must believe that he exists and that he rewards those who earnestly seek him *(Hebrews 11:5-6)*.

Reader 3: My name is Noah. During my lifetime, people became very wicked, and this grieved the Lord and filled his heart with pain. But I found favor with the Lord. He told me to build an ark of cypress wood to save myself and my family from the flood he would bring to destroy all the people on earth. The Lord made a covenant with me and told me to bring two of every kind of living creature on board the ark, and I did just as the Lord commanded. People probably thought I was crazy, but when the flood came, my family and the animals were safe while every other living thing on earth died. When it was all over, the Lord promised me he would never again destroy every living thing on earth, and he sent a rainbow as a sign of that covenant.

Handout

Narrator 4: "By faith, Noah, when warned about things not yet seen, in holy fear built an ark to save his family. By his faith he condemned the world and became heir of the righteousness that comes by faith" *(Hebrews 11:7)*.

Reader 4: My name is Abraham. I was called Abram when the Lord told me to leave my country and my people. He said he would lead me to a new land that he would make into a great nation. So although I was an old man of seventy-five, I took my wife, Sarai, and my nephew, Lot, and set out for the land of Canaan. The Lord gave this land to me and my descendants. I was faithful to God and did what he told me to do, and wherever I went, I always built an altar to him. When I was ninety-nine years old, God established a covenant with me, promising to be my God and the God of my descendants. He changed my name to Abraham and my wife's to Sarah, and he blessed us with a son, Isaac.

God continued to test me in my life. He asked me to offer Isaac as a burnt offering to him. I did as I was told, and just as I was about to kill my son with a knife, an angel of the Lord stopped me. God provided a ram for me to sacrifice instead. The Lord blessed me for my faithfulness.

Narrator 5: "By faith Abraham, when called to go to a place he would later receive as his inheritance, obeyed and went, even though he did not know where he was going. By faith he made his home in the promised land like a stranger in a foreign country; he lived in tents, as did Isaac and Jacob, who were heirs with him of the same promise. For he was looking forward to the city with foundations, whose architect and builder is God" *(Hebrews 11:8-11)*.

Narrator 6: "By faith Abraham, even though he was past age—and Sarah herself was barren—was enabled to become a father because he considered him faithful who had made the promise. And so from this one man, and he as good as dead, came descendants as numerous as the stars in the sky and as countless as the sand on the seashore" *(Hebrews 11:11-12)*.

Narrator 7: "By faith Abraham, when God tested him, offered Isaac as a sacrifice. He who had received the promises was about to sacrifice his one and only son, even though God had said to him, "It is through Isaac that your offspring will be reckoned' " *(Hebrews 11:17-18)*.

Narrator 8: "All these people were still living by faith when they died. They did not receive the things promised; they only saw them and welcomed them from a distance. And they admitted that they were aliens and strangers on earth...Instead, they were longing for a better country—a heavenly one. Therefore God is not ashamed to be called their God, for he has prepared a city for them" *(Hebrews 11:13-14, 16)*.

The Runner:
A Creative Reading

Narrator 1: Consider the long-distance runner. Consider his training, his daily commitment, his consistency, his inner drive to win the race.

Mark: My name is Mark. I'm a Christian. I'm growing spiritually and understanding more about what it means to love Jesus. I read my Bible regularly, go to church, and try to grow in faith every day.

Narrator 2: Consider the runner's discipline. She pushes herself to run every day, working harder each day than she did the day before.

Lisa: My name is Lisa. I'm a Christian. I'm relying on the Holy Spirit to make me more like Jesus every day. I pray and seek God's will for my life so I won't get caught up in temptation.

Narrator 3: The runner's coach is ready to challenge him to work harder and discipline him if necessary. The coach knows his runner has to give 100 percent every day to meet his goals.

Mark: Jesus is my guide, reminding me of my purpose in life and encouraging me to live for him.

Narrator 4: The runner begins the race with strength and confidence.

Lisa: I am forgiven and loved by God!

Narrator 5: But then someone she thought would be slower passes her by...

Lisa: Why does he seem so much more at peace than I am? Has God abandoned me?

Narrator 6: Halfway through the race, the runner grows tired.

Mark: I don't know if I should even bother reading my Bible anymore. Sometimes it's so hard to understand! And God seems so far away.

Narrator 7: The runner becomes distracted and falls down.

Lisa: I can't believe I fell into that old sin again.

Narrator 8: The runner tries to catch a glimpse of the finish line but can't see it and grows discouraged.

Mark: Live for eternity? I have to get through next week first!

Narrator 9: Suddenly the runner feels a gentle, guiding hand on her arm.

Lisa: Jesus, do you really still love me?

Narrator 10: The coach reminds the runner of his goal: to run his best and finish the race.

Mark: Jesus, I'm sorry I lost sight of you.

Narrator 11: And all the runners who have already finished the race gather to cheer.

Narrator 12: The runner picks up the pace, running again with strength and confidence, remembering the coach's words of encouragement and instruction.

Hebrews

by step, the runner commands his or her legs to keep moving toward the finish line.

Let's explore this image further with a creative reading.

Give each person a photocopy of "The Runner: A Creative Reading" handout. Assign readers to read the narrator roles and the parts of Mark and Lisa. If you have more teenagers than parts, form some pairs to read narrator parts together.

Lead teenagers in the creative reading, then close in prayer.

Scripture: Hebrews 13:1-8

Theme: Serving others

Experience: In this **service opportunity**, teenagers will find practical ways to put their faith into action.

Preparation: You'll need Bibles, white paper, construction paper, staplers, pens or pencils, an offering plate or basket, tape or tacks, and large star-shaped stickers.

Worship

Have teenagers form groups of three or four. Distribute Bibles, and have someone in each group read aloud Hebrews 13:1-8. Then say:

> This passage contains lots of practical advice for putting your faith into action. And that's just what we're going to do! In your group, agree on an idea from this passage that will be the basis of a service project you'll commit to doing.
>
> As a group, decide what service project you'd like to perform. Then write and sign a simple contract explaining what role each of you will play in carrying out your project. Make sure your contract includes a completion date that's no more than a month away.
>
> We'll display the contracts, so mount your contract on a piece of colored construction paper. When you've accomplished your goal, we'll put a star on the contract. When all groups have completed their projects, we'll have a class celebration.

Distribute paper, construction paper, staplers, and pens or pencils. Have each group develop a service idea, write the idea as a contract on a half sheet of white paper, sign the contract, and staple it to a sheet of construction paper. Circulate among the groups to offer help and encouragement as needed. If teenagers seem stumped, suggest the following ideas based on the Scripture passage:

● Volunteer in a homeless shelter or soup kitchen (verses 1-2).

● Write letters of encouragement to people in prison (verse 3).

● Collect toys or gifts for prisoners to give their children or family members on visiting day (verse 3).

● Send care packages to missionaries and people who live in war-torn countries (verse 3b).

● Commit to giving up a luxury and sending the money you save to a local charity or to your church's mission work instead (verse 5).

● Commit to praying for church leaders every day, asking God to guide them in their decision making (verse 7).

● Write letters of encouragement to church leaders, or plan a thank you party for them (verse 7).

When teenagers have finished making their contracts, say:

As a way of dedicating your projects to the Lord, I'm going to pass around this offering plate. Place your contract in the plate as your offering to God.

Pass an offering plate or basket to the first group, then have a member of the first group carry the basket to the second group, and so on. When all the contracts have been offered to God, close with a group prayer asking God to bless your teenagers as they strive to serve him.

After class, post the contracts in your meeting area. Each week, ask teenagers how their service projects are coming, and encourage them to abide by their contracts. As each group finishes its project, place a large star-shaped sticker on the contract. When all groups have completed their projects, celebrate a job well done with an ice cream or pizza party!

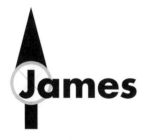

James

Scripture: James 1:17-27

Theme: Faith in action

Experience: In this **artistic experience**, teenagers will make reminders that faith without action is worthless.

Preparation: You'll need Bibles, scrap paper, blank self-stick labels, pens or pencils, calligraphy pens and samples, small stencils (try to include some sports stencils), stencil paints and brushes, and a travel mirror with a stand for each person.

James

Worship

Have teenagers form a circle. Distribute Bibles and have a volunteer read James 1:17-27 aloud as others read along. Then have pairs of teenagers discuss the following questions. Ask:

● Which part of this passage really jumps out at you?

● Have you ever made a resolution and then not followed through on it? Explain.

● How is failing to follow through on a resolution different from not following the advice in the Bible? How is it similar?

Say: **It's one thing to fail to follow through on a personal resolution, but it's a far more serious thing not to follow the advice of the Bible. It's important to try every day to keep our words and actions in line with the Bible. To help us do that, we're going to make reminders today.**

This Bible passage says that not doing what the Bible says is like looking in a mirror, then forgetting what you look like. So today we're going to make mirror memory frames. The design will be totally up to you. Here's how it works.

Explain that each teenager should choose one verse from the Bible passage as the verse he or she wants to be reminded of every day. Teenagers can write the verses in whatever styles they choose. Point out the calligraphy samples, and let teenagers use scrap paper to practice the styles of writing they like.

When teenagers feel confident in their writing, have each person copy a verse onto a blank self-stick label and place the label in the center of a mirror. Teenagers can decorate the area around the verses in whatever manner they choose, using stencils and paints or painting designs freehand.

When teenagers have finished making their mirror memory frames, have them form a circle.

Say: **As a way of dedicating our mirrors and our hearts to God, let's have a short dedication ceremony. As we go around the circle, read the verse on your mirror aloud, then place your mirror on the floor in front of you as you say a short prayer, asking the Holy Spirit to guide and work in your life. You may pray aloud or silently.**

Encourage teenagers to place the frames in their rooms, near the mirrors they look in every day, to remind them of what the Bible says.

Scripture: James 2:1-17

Theme: Favoritism

Experience: In this **dramatic presentation**, teenagers will illustrate the difference between showing favoritism and loving their neighbors as themselves.

Preparation: You'll need a Bible, a photocopy of the "Favoritism Flops" skit (p. 96) for each person, and six or more hand mirrors.

Worship

Read James 2:1-17 aloud. Then tell students they'll be performing a dramatic presentation to illustrate God's truth in James 2:1-17. Ask for three volunteers to be the wealthy, three volunteers to be the poor, one volunteer to be the greeter, and one volunteer to be the narrator. Be sure each student has a part; you can add wealthy people, poor people, or narrators.

Before the skit, open a Bible to James 2, and place the Bible on the floor to one side of the stage.

To begin, three wealthy people and three poor people should form a single-file line at one end of the room, with the wealthy people at the front of the line. The wealthy should hold their heads and shoulders high; the poor should slump their shoulders and droop their heads. The greeter should stand in the middle of the room with his or her back turned to the line. Give each of the three wealthy people and the three poor people a hand mirror.

Have teenagers practice the skit several times until they're ready to perform it for another group or for the congregation.

Scripture: James 3:13-18

Theme: Wisdom

Experience: In this **creative reading** and **prayer of petition**, teenagers will contrast earthly wisdom and spiritual wisdom, then ask God for spiritual wisdom.

Preparation: You'll need a photocopy of the "Seeking Wisdom" script (p. 97-98) for each person.

Worship

Have teenagers sit in a circle, and give each person a photocopy of the "Seeking Wisdom" script. Assign a narrator and six speakers. Then have the remaining teenagers form four groups, and assign groups to read for Group 1, Group 2, Group 3, and Group 4. Then have teenagers read through the creative reading as worship to God.

After the creative reading, lead teenagers in the following prayer, giving

Favoritism Flops

(based on James 2:1-17)

(As the Narrator speaks, the Wealthy move forward, one by one, to the center of the room. They walk with large strides and with their heads held high. As they reach the center of the room, the Greeter turns excitedly, shakes their hands, and pretends to take pictures.)

Narrator: Some people command attention and respect. In our society, it's the rich, the beautiful, and the famous. We take photographs of them and ask for their autographs. We read about them; we wear what they wear; we buy the products they recommend. We give them special treatment.

(The Wealthy freeze in place.)

(Next, as the Narrator speaks, the Poor move forward, one by one, to stand next to the Wealthy. They walk with small, tired steps and with their heads down. The Greeter avoids them and gives them nasty looks.)

Narrator: Then there are the people we seem to forget: the poor, the plain, and the anonymous. We pass them every day without noticing. And when we do notice, it's often with displeasure. Maybe we blame them for their misfortune. Maybe we feel uncomfortable, even guilty.

(The Poor freeze in place.)

(The Greeter picks up the Bible and reads aloud James 2:1-4.)

(As the Narrator speaks, the Greeter walks to and looks at each person.)

Narrator: When we treat people differently, we're judging. We're saying that wealth or beauty or fame makes a good person, while poverty, plainness, or anonymity makes a bad person. But the Bible says that, instead of judging, we're to be merciful just as we want others to be merciful to us.

(Each time the Narrator says, "Love your neighbor as yourself," the Greeter walks to the next person, who holds up a mirror to reflect the Greeter's face. Then the Greeter smiles warmly and shakes that person's hand.)

Narrator: Again and again, the Bible says, "Love your neighbor as yourself." *(Narrator repeats "Love your neighbor as yourself" for each Wealthy and Poor person.)* When you do, you're not only professing your faith, but acting upon it.

Seeking Wisdom

(based on James 3:13-18)

Narrator: Who is wise and understanding among you?

Speaker 1: I am! I built my own business from nothing; now I employ two hundred employees.

Speaker 2: I am! I'm a professor of physics, so I understand how the universe functions.

Speaker 3: I am! As a senator, I help to determine the direction the entire nation should take.

Narrator: Understanding is shown by a life lived well; wisdom, by deeds done in humility.

Speaker 1: Oh, I'm humble! Let me tell you how humble I am...

Speaker 2: Your definition is interesting, but relatively speaking...

Speaker 3: I doubt that's what the people think! I debate your point...

Narrator: Who is wise and understanding among you?

Speaker 4: My folks work really hard to give us a good life. They're never too busy to steer us in the right direction, though, and they're never too tired to show us how much they love us.

Speaker 5: I have this teacher who always stays late to help me figure out my algebra homework.

Speaker 6: My friend is always looking out for others. She's the kind of person who will drop anything to help someone in trouble.

Narrator: There are two kinds of wisdom. Earthly wisdom says...

Group 1: Keep up with the Joneses.

Narrator: Spiritual wisdom says...

Group 2: Be glad for others.

Narrator: Earthly wisdom says...

Group 3: There's no absolute truth.

Narrator: Spiritual wisdom says...

Handout

Group 4: Jesus is the truth, and the truth will set you free.

Narrator: Earthly wisdom says...

Group 1: Win at any cost.

Narrator: Spiritual wisdom says...

Group 2: Blessed are the peacemakers.

Group 3: Seek peace and pursue it.

Narrator: Earthly wisdom says...

Group 4: Look out for number one.

Narrator: Spiritual wisdom says...

Group 1: Love your neighbor as yourself.

Group 2: Take the nature of a servant.

Narrator: Earthly wisdom says...

Group 3: Make them pay!

Narrator: Spiritual wisdom says...

Group 4: Mercy triumphs over judgment.

Group 1: Forgive and you will be forgiven.

Narrator: Earthly wisdom says...

Group 2: Join the winning team.

Narrator: Spiritual wisdom says...

Group 3: Be impartial and sincere.

Groups 1 and 2: Earthly wisdom brings disorder.

Groups 3 and 4: Spiritual wisdom brings righteousness.

Narrator: There are two kinds of wisdom. Earthly wisdom says...

Groups 1, 2, 3, and 4: "It's all about me!"

Narrator: Spiritual wisdom says...

Groups 1, 2, 3, and 4: "It's all about God."

each person in the circle a chance to complete each sentence aloud. Be sure to complete each sentence yourself as an example for teenagers.

Pray: **God, we need your wisdom to know the difference between...**

We need your wisdom when we struggle with...

We need your wisdom to remind us that...

God, thank you for showing us the difference between earthly wisdom and spiritual wisdom. Amen.

1 Peter

Scripture: 1 Peter 1:3-9

Theme: Hope

Experience: In this **act of praise, artistic experience,** and **musical experience,** teenagers will illustrate the praise and promises of Scripture in a mural.

Preparation: You'll need newsprint or poster board, tape, markers in a variety of colors, Bibles, a CD or cassette of praise music, and a CD or cassette player.

Before the experience, tape a large sheet of newsprint or pieces of poster board to a wall in your youth room. Label the newsprint or poster board with these five headings, leaving enough space under each one for teenagers to illustrate each idea: "Praise be to God for a living hope," "Inheritance of heaven," "Suffer grief in all kinds of trials," "Faith proved genuine," and "Glorious joy: salvation." If you have a large group, you may want to do several sets of murals.

Worship

Have students form groups of three or four, and be sure each group has a Bible. If you have a small class, let everyone work together as one group.

Say: **Today we're going to read a Scripture from 1 Peter that sounds like a hymn of praise to God. These verses praise God for**

1 Peter

giving us the living hope, through the death and resurrection of Jesus Christ, that we will inherit the promise of heaven and salvation. After we read this Scripture in our groups, we'll work together to illustrate these words. I'm going to play some inspirational music while you create your mural of praise.

Have groups read 1 Peter 1:3-9 and take a few minutes to discuss how to illustrate the Scripture under the words you have posted on the newsprint or poster board. Then make markers available, and start the praise music. Have groups begin working on different parts of the mural and move to new sections every few minutes at your signal. Allow them to refer to the Scripture for ideas.

When the mural is finished, have groups take turns explaining some of their drawings and how they relate to the Scripture passage. Close the worship time by singing a hymn of praise together and admiring the artistic impressions created by the group.

Scripture: 1 Peter 1:17-23

Theme: Imperishable goals
Experience: In this sharing time, teenagers will set imperishable goals for the future.
Preparation: You'll need Bibles.

Worship

Have teenagers form pairs. Distribute Bibles and ask each pair to read 1 Peter 1:17-23. Then ask:

● What's the difference between perishable and imperishable things?
● What things do you personally have that are perishable? imperishable?
● If you could accomplish only one thing in your life before you die, what would it be?

Say: As a way to worship God, let's set imperishable goals for the future. An imperishable goal is one that makes a difference that lasts for eternity. It's an investment in God's kingdom.

Encourage teenagers to share their goals with their partners. Then ask volunteers to share their goals with the group.

Say: In the Bible passage, Peter instructs us to "have sincere love for your brothers, love one another deeply, from the heart." Take two or three minutes to discuss the following questions with your partner:

● How will the particular goal you chose accomplish the Bible's instruction to love one another?
● What are some imperishable things God has already done in your life?

1 Peter

After two or three minutes, have teenagers form a circle and join hands as you pray that God will give them strength, courage, and grace to accomplish their imperishable goals.

Scripture: 1 Peter 5:6-11

Theme: Self-control

Experience: In this **prayer of confession**, teenagers will strengthen their awareness of the need for self-control and seek God's forgiveness for the times they have failed. This experience is best done outdoors in an area with lots of trees, bushes, and plants. Choose an area where students can pull up a plant or two.

Preparation: You'll need a Bible, index cards, and pens or pencils.

Worship

Ask a teenager to read 1 Peter 5:6-11 aloud. Then say:

This passage tells us that as Christians we must be "self-controlled," "alert," and "firm in the faith." Ask:

● How can we demonstrate self-control in our lives?

● How do we often show that we don't have self-control in our lives?

Have the teenagers follow you as you lead them through an outdoor area. Locate a small wild plant, and ask for a volunteer to pluck it.

Next find a larger plant, and have another volunteer pull it up. (This should be slightly more difficult.)

Locate a medium-sized bush, and ask for a volunteer to try to pull it out of the ground. (This will probably be impossible to do.)

Finally, find a large tree, and ask for a fourth volunteer to try to pull it up. Ask:

● What were the main differences you noticed among these four plants?

● What made the tree impossible to pull out of the ground?

● How are the roots of the tree similar to self-control in our lives?

● How can we become stronger and more rooted in our lives?

Say: If we have self-control, it's much easier to resist the devil who "prowls around like a roaring lion looking for someone to devour."

Give each person a pen or pencil and an index card. Instruct teenagers to find separate trees that are solidly rooted and to sit beneath them.

Say: On your card, draw one small plant, one larger plant, a bush, and a tree all in a row down one side of the card. Next to each plant and the bush, write a brief description of a time you were like the weaker plants and showed no self-control. Beside the tree, describe a time you demonstrated self-control. When you've finished, draw another tree, and describe an area in your life in which you would like

to develop more self-control. There is no need to write your name on the card. When you've finished, you may want to spend a few minutes in silent prayer, confessing your struggles with self-control to God. After approximately ten minutes, bring your card back to this location.

When the teenagers have returned, ask for a volunteer to gather the cards without looking at them. Have that person pray over the requests, asking both for forgiveness for the lack of self-control and for strength to develop self-control in areas of need.

Take the cards after the prayer, and assure the teenagers that the cards will be destroyed.

2 Peter

Scripture: 2 Peter 1:16-21

Theme: God's work

Experience: In this **prayer of thanksgiving** and **sharing time,** teenagers will share stories of God's work in their lives.

Preparation: You'll need a Bible.

Before the experience, set a chair at the front of the meeting area.

Worship

Have teenagers sit facing the chair you set up before the experience. Ask a volunteer to read aloud 2 Peter 1:16-21.

Say: **When an eyewitness testifies at a courtroom trial, that testimony is powerful evidence. Similarly, our stories about our own experiences are powerful evidence about God's work in our lives.**

Let's thank God by "testifying" about what he's done for us. Maybe God healed a broken friendship or gave you the discipline to study regularly. Think of something God has done for you, and you'll get a turn on our "witness stand."

As each person takes a turn on the witness stand, act as a "lawyer," asking questions about the situation, God's involvement, and the outcome. Don't forget to take your turn and encourage the teenagers to ask you questions.

After everyone has had a turn, say:

What wonderful examples of what God does in our lives. Let's pray to thank God.

Have each person take a turn thanking God for what he's done in his or her life, then close by praying:

God, thank you for these eyewitnesses to your love. We praise you for all you've done for us. Amen.

1 John

9-13-02 Youth Group.

Scripture: 1 John 1:1–2:2

Theme: Walking in the light

Experience: In this **prayer of confession** and **sharing time**, teenagers will simulate the light of Jesus in their lives.

Preparation: You'll need a Bible; a small candle with a drip catcher for each person, including you; and matches.

Worship

Give each person a candle, keeping one for yourself. Have teenagers form a circle, and turn off all the lights to make the room as dark as possible. Ask students to sit silently for one minute.

After one minute, light your candle.

Say: **A ray of light will always penetrate darkness. Even in this room, with this small amount of light, we can see much more clearly when the candle is lit. A "ray" of darkness has no effect on light. Listen to these words.**

Read 1 John 1:1–2:2 slowly and clearly. Then ask:

● How is God light?

● What are some examples of how a person might walk in darkness

1 John

while proclaiming to be a follower of Jesus?

● Why can't we ever be free from sin?

● Why do you suppose confession is an important part of being forgiven?

Say: Everybody in this room has fallen into sin. All of us in this room will continue to fall into sin until we die or Jesus takes us up to heaven. The light of Jesus conquers sin every time, in any situation, just as the candle always overcomes the darkness. But sometimes we choose not to walk in the light.

The light of Jesus purifies us and makes us worthy to be in the presence of the Lord. This Scripture passage says, "God is light; in him there is no darkness...If we walk in the light, as he is in the light, we have fellowship with one another, and the blood of Jesus, his Son, purifies us from all sin...If we confess our sins, he is faithful and just and will forgive us our sins and purify us from all unrighteousness." If you're a Christian—a sinner who has faith in the death and resurrection of Jesus—his light lives in you.

Light the candle of the person next to you, and ask students to pass the candle's light from one person to the next. When all the candles are lit, say:

We are not alone. Just as our small candles are lighting up this room, Jesus' light shines through all Christians.

Spend several minutes in prayer. Encourage teenagers to confess their sins publicly if they feel the Holy Spirit calling them to do so. Otherwise, ask them to confess their sins silently. After several minutes, close with this prayer:

Dear Jesus, please shine your light through us. And help us not to cover up that light with sin. Instead, help us to repent from that sin so it may never separate us from your fellowship again. Amen.

Scripture: 1 John 3:1-24

Theme: Love

Experience: In this musical experience, teenagers will write a song about God's love.

Preparation: You'll need Bibles, paper, and pens or pencils.

Worship

Say: As you know, love is a very important theme in the Bible. It's so prevalent, in fact, that we may rush over it instead of really reading and internalizing what God is saying to us. To help us break out of that pattern, we're going to write a song today—a love song.

Have teenagers form four groups. Give each group Bibles, paper, and pens or pencils. Assign the first group to read 1 John 3:1-6; the second group, 1 John 3:7-12; the third group, 1 John 3:13-20; and the fourth group, 1 John 3:21-24.

Say: **In your group, read the Scripture. As you read, try to decipher what it's saying about God's love for us or our Christlike love for others. Ask one another questions about the Scripture to get to the most basic element of what it's saying about love. Some of your verses may seem difficult to relate to love initially, but they all do.**

After a few minutes, say:

Now we need to decide what tune to use for our love song. Keeping in mind that we're praising God, let's choose a tune.

Have teenagers brainstorm tunes to use until the teenagers have agreed on one.

Then say: **Now each group is going to write a verse of the song. Write your verse to praise God for his love, keeping in mind the Scripture your group read. Try to use your own words so your verse is really communication from you to God.**

Distribute paper and pencils to everyone, and circulate to help groups as needed. After a few minutes, say:

Now it's time to hear our love song!

Have the groups stand up in order from the first group to the fourth group, and have them perform their verses in order.

When everyone has performed, have the whole group applaud everyone's effort. If teenagers want to, have them sing their love song again. Close the experience by leading everyone in a harmonious "amen."

Scripture: 1 John 4:7-12

Theme: Service

Experience: In this **service opportunity**, teenagers will serve the church.

Preparation: You'll need a bag of microwavable popcorn, access to a microwave oven, a cardboard box, Bibles, and a list of minor jobs at the church your group can do in thirty minutes.

Just before the experience, pop a bag of microwavable popcorn, and place it in a cardboard box. Loosely seal the box so the smell will seep out of the box. Place the box in a corner of your meeting area.

Worship

When everyone has arrived, say:

1 John

I don't know about you, but I'm hungry.

Excuse yourself from the room, and take the box of popcorn with you. Wait outside the room for a few seconds, and then return.

Say: **Wow. I feel better.**

Ask teenagers to shout out ideas of what they think is inside the box. Students will know what you've been carrying around. Ask:

● **How did you know what was in the box?**
● **How did my actions convince you that I had something to eat?**

Say: **There's a definite correlation between what we believe and how we behave. What we believe can determine how we act. In fact, what we believe fuels our actions. For example, I'll bet that when you saw me leaving the room to eat this popcorn, you wanted some. Because you believed I had popcorn in this box, you behaved in a certain way.**

Ask teenagers to form groups of three and read 1 John 4:7-12 in their groups. When they've read the Scripture, ask groups to discuss these questions:

● **How does sacrificing something show love?**
● **Can love be invisible? Explain.**

Say: **This passage makes one thing very clear—our identity as Christians is revealed by how we love others. If we can love each other, those who don't know Jesus will see our love and know what we believe and who we believe in.**

Explain to the teenagers that they're about to put this passage into action as a way to worship God. Gather teenagers in the center of your meeting space, and say a short prayer for the service projects the group will do.

Lead your teenagers in completing as many tasks as possible on your list of jobs.

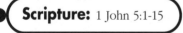

Scripture: 1 John 5:1-15

Theme: Faith

Experience: In this **sharing time**, teenagers will share their faith stories with the rest of the congregation.

Preparation: You'll need Bibles, a video camera, a photocopy of the "Faith Questionnaire" handout (p. 107) for each person, and pens or pencils.

Before the experience, get permission from your church leadership to produce a video about your teenagers' faith and present it to the congregation.

Faith
Questionnaire

On a scale of 1 to 5 (with 1 meaning no faith and 5 meaning ultimate faith), record how much faith you have that each of the following statements is true.

The sun will come up tomorrow.

You will be alive tomorrow.

You will no longer have to go to school someday.

Your parents teach you the truth about everything.

Your teachers teach you the truth about everything.

The earth was created by God.

Jonah survived inside a fish for three days as he prayed to God.

Methuselah lived 969 years.

Sarah gave birth to Isaac at the age of ninety.

Jesus rose from the dead.

Jesus turned water into wine.

Jesus fed five thousand people with two fish and five loaves of bread.

Jude

Worship

Give each person a "Faith Questionnaire" handout and a pen or pencil, and ask teenagers to fill out the questionnaires. Then have teenagers form groups of two or three and discuss what they've written.

When each person has had an opportunity to share his or her answers, gather teenagers again and ask:

● How do you define the word "faith"?

● What are some of the things you have faith in?

● What are some of the things you struggle to have faith in?

● What needs to happen before you can comfortably have faith in something?

After some discussion, read 1 John 5:1-15 aloud. Ask:

● Is the type of faith that is identified here any different from the type of faith we have been discussing? Explain.

● If we choose to have faith in Jesus, how do we change in the eyes of God?

Say: **People can benefit from knowing about our faith. Other members of the church will benefit from our faith if we share it with them. We have permission to produce a video about our faith and present it to the congregation. We can be as creative as we'd like to be. We need to make sure that it's based on truth, that it uplifts the name of Jesus, and that it lasts ten minutes or less. Let's re-examine the Scripture and come up with a plan together.**

Guide students in the production of the video. Then play the tape for the congregation.

Jude

Scripture: Jude 17-25

Theme: Perseverance

Experience: In this celebration of the Lord's Supper and service opportunity, teenagers will celebrate fellowship with the Lord and commit to showing God's mercy and love to others.

Preparation: You'll need a Bible and elements for the Lord's Supper. Before the experience, arrange for a member of the clergy to preside over the Lord's Supper if necessary.

Worship

Have youth stand in a circle and hold the wrists of the people next to them (to create a stronger link than just holding hands). Stand in the center of the circle and say:

Remember when you played the game Red Rover as children? You held hands with your team and tried to hang on so no one could burst through your line. That was one example of perseverance, or a continued, patient effort. Jude 17-25 is about perseverance. Listen.

Read Jude 17-25 aloud. Then repeat the line

"These are the men who divide you, who...do not have the Spirit."

As you say this, try to break apart a few of the linked wrists in your group. Then say:

"But you...build yourselves up in your most holy faith and pray in the Holy Spirit."

Say: Imagine yourselves building a circle of faith together. Pray in the Spirit that your fellowship with the Lord will hold against those who would divide you. Together you can persevere. Now feel yourselves surrounded in God's love as you await his mercy to bring you to eternal life. Let's celebrate the Lord's Supper together.

Celebrate the Lord's Supper together according to the custom in your church. When you've finished, gather everyone and reread Jude 22-23. Brainstorm a service project your group can do together to show God's love and mercy to others.

Revelation

Scripture: Revelation 5:11-14

Theme: Praise

Experience: In this **act of praise, creative movement,** and **musical experience,** teenagers will praise God creatively.

Preparation: You'll need a Bible; a CD or cassette of an upbeat praise song; a CD or cassette player; and everyday objects found in your meeting area or church, such as cups, spoons, books, ribbons, streamers, and anything else that can be used to make noise or motion to music.

Worship

Ask: **What are some ways we can praise God?**

After students share some ideas, ask someone to read Revelation 5:11-14 aloud.

Say: **This is a small part of John's description of his vision of heaven in Revelation. Imagine the voices of "thousands upon thousands, and ten thousand times ten thousand" angels encircling the throne of God and singing his praises. And if you can imagine that, listen to verse 13 again: "Then I heard every creature in heaven and on earth and under the earth and on the sea, and all that is in them, singing" God's praises.**

Today we're going to praise God with whatever we can find in this room.

(Or you may specify whatever they can find in the church, or you can do this activity outside and let teenagers choose objects outdoors.) Give youth a few minutes to find objects they can use as instruments to play or objects to wave or twirl in praise.

Choose an upbeat praise song, such as "Awesome God," or something like the "Hallelujah Chorus" from Handel's *Messiah*.

Tell teenagers that when the music starts, they are to move creatively to the music and make noise or motions with their objects. When you call their names, they are to shout out something they would like to praise God for. If they're really getting into it, play another song and keep the praises going!

Scripture: Revelation 7:9-17

Theme: Heaven

Experience: In this **artistic experience**, teenagers will draw a mural depicting what they think heaven will be like.

Preparation: You'll need newsprint, tape, colored markers, and Bibles.

Before the experience, tape several large sheets of newsprint together to make a mural background. Then make three more mural backgrounds. Tape each mural background to a separate wall, with the taped sides against the wall. Set out a variety of colored markers near each mural background.

Worship

Have teenagers form four groups, and give each group a Bible. Have teenagers read Revelation 7:9-17 in their groups. Then have each group go to a separate mural background. Have teenagers in each group work together to create a mural depicting the passage they just read. Encourage teenagers to refer to the Bible often to look for details they think should be included.

When groups have finished drawing, have them present their murals to each other, one at a time. Make sure to affirm each group after its presentation. Then ask:

● What do you think will be the coolest part of heaven?
● What are you most looking forward to about heaven?
● What's one question you want to ask God when you get there?
● How do you know you're going to go to heaven?

Say: **We know from the Bible that there's only one way into heaven and that's faith in Jesus.** Look at your mural. Look at all the people around the throne. Ask:

● What would it be like to be included in this picture?

Ask teenagers to go to their murals and sign their names somewhere on the pictures. Then have students form a circle in the center of the room and face outward. Distribute Bibles, and have teenagers read Revelation 7:10, 12 in unison. Then collect the Bibles, and have teenagers hold hands. Ask youth to pray silently, thanking God for preparing a place for all his children.

After the worship experience, you may want to encourage teenagers to speak with you if they aren't sure they're going to heaven.

Scripture: Revelation 21:1-6

Theme: Jesus' return

Experience: In this **creative reading**, teenagers will affirm the power and majesty of God.

Revelation

Preparation: You'll need Bibles and a photocopy of the "New Heaven and Earth" creative reading (p. 113) for each person.

Worship

Say: **When we think about time in reference to eternity, the amount of time we spend here on earth is very brief. After we die, we'll not only have eternal fellowship with God, but we'll also have a place to dwell with other believers.**

Have teenagers read Revelation 21:1-6 aloud together. Then ask:

● How did our reading of this passage aloud communicate the intensity of what was being said?

● Why does this text work well as a dramatic reading?

● How would this world look if there were no death or no pain?

● When God said, "It is done," what was he referring to?

Give each person a copy of the "New Heaven and Earth" creative reading and say:

The passage we read earlier explained a reformation that's going to take place at some point. What it will be like and how it will affect us are beyond our imagination. Let's read this passage again using the handout and try to capture the intensity of what's being said. We'll read it as a prayer, praising God for what he has created and what he will soon create. After the reading is finished, we'll move right into open prayer, and then I'll offer a closing prayer.

Lead students in the creative reading, then close in prayer, asking God to help everyone look forward to Jesus' return.

Scripture: Revelation 22:12-21

Theme: Jesus' return

Experience: In this **act of praise** and **celebration of the Lord's Supper**, teenagers will look forward to Jesus' return.

Preparation: You'll need one photocopy of the "Revelation Passages" handout (p. 115), scissors, Bibles, and elements for the Lord's Supper.

Before the experience, cut apart the sections of the "Revelation Passages" handout, and ask someone to lead praise music for the group. If necessary, invite a member of the clergy to serve the Lord's Supper at the appropriate time.

New Heaven and Earth

Leader: "Then I saw a new heaven and a new earth, for the first heaven and the first earth had passed away, and there was no longer any sea."

Group: "But in keeping with his promise we are looking forward to a new heaven and a new earth, the home of righteousness" (2 Peter 3:13).

Leader: "I saw the Holy City, the new Jerusalem, coming down out of heaven from God, prepared as a bride beautifully dressed for her husband."

Group: "Awake, Awake, O Zion, clothe yourself with strength. Put on your garments of splendor, O Jerusalem, the holy city. The uncircumcised and defiled will not enter you again" (Isaiah 52:1).

Leader: "And I heard a loud voice from the throne saying, 'Now the dwelling of God is with men, and he will live with them. They will be his people, and God himself will be with them and be their God.' "

Group: " 'Shout and be glad, O Daughter of Zion. For I am coming, and I will live among you,' declares the Lord" (Zechariah 2:10).

Leader: "He will wipe every tear from their eyes. There will be no more death or mourning or crying or pain, for the old order of things has passed away."

Group: "They will enter Zion with singing; everlasting joy will crown their heads. Gladness and joy will overtake them, and sorrow and sighing will flee away" (Isaiah 35:10).

Leader: "He who was seated on the throne said, 'I am making everything new!' Then he said, 'Write this down, for these words are trustworthy and true.' "

Group: "Then I saw a great white throne and him who was seated on it. Earth and sky fled from his presence, and there was no place for them" (Revelation 20:11).

Leader: "He said to me: 'It is done. I am the Alpha and the Omega, the Beginning and the End. To him who is thirsty I will give to drink without cost from the spring of the water of life.' "

Group: "Jesus answered her, 'If you knew the gift of God and who it is that asks you for a drink, you would have asked him and he would have given you living water' " (John 4:10).

All: "Behold, I am coming soon!" (Revelation 22:7a).

Revelation

Worship

Have teenagers form pairs.

Say: **I'd like you to shut your eyes, forget about the people around you, and focus on God for the next few minutes. I'm going to say some words. After I say a word, I'd like you to tell your partner the first thing that comes into your mind. Ready? Here goes.**

Say the following words, allowing time for teenagers to share after each one:

Reward. Blessing. Homecoming. Resurrection. A good friend.

When you've read the words, ask teenagers to share some of their reactions with the rest of the group.

Say: **Have you ever thought about what Jesus' return will be like? When Jesus returns, it will be like those things you just thought about, but it will be so much more amazing. Let's spend the next few minutes reading Jesus' promise to come back and praising him for his return.**

Give the sections from the "Revelation Passages" handout to six students. Have your music leader begin to play music softly while you begin the praise time with a short prayer.

Ask the student with the first section to read the passage. Then have your music leader lead a praise song. After the song, ask the student with the second section to read that passage. Follow the passage with another praise song. Continue until the six Scripture passages have each been read and followed by a song.

When you've finished the last song, read Revelation 22:20 aloud.

Say: **One way to celebrate Jesus' future return is through the Lord's Supper. Doing this not only causes us to remember his death, but also acts as a celebration of our hope.**

Celebrate the Lord's Supper together. Then read Revelation 22:21, and close with a short prayer.

Revelation
Passages

1. "Behold, I am coming soon! My reward is with me, and I will give to everyone according to what he has done. I am the Alpha and the Omega, the First and the Last, the Beginning and the End" (Revelation 22:12-13).

2. "Blessed are those who wash their robes, that they may have the right to the tree of life and may go through the gates into the city. Outside are the dogs, those who practice magic arts, the sexually immoral, the murderers, the idolaters and everyone who loves and practices falsehood" (Revelation 22:14-15).

3. "I, Jesus, have sent my angel to give you this testimony for the churches. I am the Root and the Offspring of David, and the bright Morning Star" (Revelation 22:16).

4. "The Spirit and the bride say, "Come!" And let him who hears say, "Come!" Whoever is thirsty, let him come; and whoever wishes, let him take the free gift of the water of life" (Revelation 22:17).

5. "I warn everyone who hears the words of the prophecy of this book: If anyone adds anything to them, God will add to him the plagues described in this book. And if anyone takes words away from this book of prophecy, God will take away from him his share in the tree of life and in the holy city, which are described in this book" (Revelation 22:18-19).

6. "He who testifies to these things says, "Yes, I am coming soon." Amen. Come, Lord Jesus. The grace of the Lord Jesus be with God's people. Amen" (Revelation 22:20-21).

Scripture Index

Scripture Index

Theme Index

Theme Index

Worship-Style Index

Worship-Style Index

Worship-Style Index

Worship-Style Index

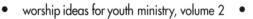

Group Publishing, Inc.
Attention: Product Development
P.O. Box 481
Loveland, CO 80539
Fax: (970) 679-4370

Evaluation for *WORSHIP IDEAS FOR YOUTH MINISTRY, VOL. 2*

Please help Group Publishing, Inc., continue to provide innovative and useful resources for ministry. Please take a moment to fill out this evaluation and mail or fax it to us. Thanks!

● ● ●

1. As a whole, this book has been (circle one)

not very helpful   very helpful

1   2   3   4   5   6   7   8   9   10

2. The best things about this book:

3. Ways this book could be improved:

4. Things I will change because of this book:

5. Other books I'd like to see Group publish in the future:

6. Would you be interested in field-testing future Group products and giving us your feedback? If so, please fill in the information below:

Name _____

Street Address _____

City _____ State _____ ZIP _____

Phone Number _____ Date_____

Bible Study Series

Give Your Teenagers a Solid Faith Foundation That Lasts a Lifetime!

Here are the *essentials* of the Christian life—core values teenagers *must* believe to make good decisions now...and build an *unshakable* lifelong faith. Developed by youth workers like you...field-tested with *real* youth groups in *real* churches...here's the meat your kids *must* have to grow spiritually—presented in a fun, involving way!

Each 4-session **Core Belief Bible Study Series** book lets you easily...
● Lead deep, compelling, *relevant* discussions your kids won't want to miss...
● Involve teenagers in exploring life-changing truths...
● Help kids create healthy relationships with each other—and you!

Plus you'll make an *eternal difference* in the lives of your kids as you give them a solid faith foundation that stands firm on God's Word.

Here are the Core Belief Bible Study Series titles already available...

Senior High Studies

Why **Authority** Matters	0-7644-0892-5
Why **Being a Christian** Matters	0-7644-0883-6
Why **Creation** Matters	0-7644-0880-1
Why **Forgiveness** Matters	0-7644-0887-9
Why **God** Matters	0-7644-0874-7
Why **God's Justice** Matters	0-7644-0886-0
Why **Jesus Christ** Matters	0-7644-0875-5
Why **Love** Matters	0-7644-0889-5
Why **Our Families** Matter	0-7644-0894-1
Why **Personal Character** Matters	0-7644-0885-2
Why **Prayer** Matters	0-7644-0893-3
Why **Relationships** Matter	0-7644-0896-8
Why **Serving Others** Matters	0-7644-0895-X
Why **Spiritual Growth** Matters	0-7644-0884-4
Why **Suffering** Matters	0-7644-0879-8
Why **the Bible** Matters	0-7644-0882-8
Why **the Church** Matters	0-7644-0890-9
Why **the Holy Spirit** Matters	0-7644-0876-3
Why **the Last Days** Matter	0-7644-0888-7
Why **the Spiritual Realm** Matters	0-7644-0881-X
Why **Worship** Matters	0-7644-0891-7

Junior High/Middle School Studies

The Truth About **Authority**	0-7644-0868-2
The Truth About **Being a Christian**	0-7644-0859-3
The Truth About **Creation**	0-7644-0856-9
The Truth About **Developing Character**	0-7644-0861-5
The Truth About **God**	0-7644-0850-X
The Truth About **God's Justice**	0-7644-0862-3
The Truth About **Jesus Christ**	0-7644-0851-8
The Truth About **Love**	0-7644-0865-8
The Truth About **Our Families**	0-7644-0870-4
The Truth About **Prayer**	0-7644-0869-0
The Truth About **Relationships**	0-7644-0872-0
The Truth About **Serving Others**	0-7644-0871-2
The Truth About **Sin and Forgiveness**	0-7644-0863-1
The Truth About **Spiritual Growth**	0-7644-0860-7
The Truth About **Suffering**	0-7644-0855-0
The Truth About **the Bible**	0-7644-0858-5
The Truth About **the Church**	0-7644-0899-2
The Truth About **the Holy Spirit**	0-7644-0852-6
The Truth About **the Last Days**	0-7644-0864-X
The Truth About **the Spiritual Realm**	0-7644-0857-7
The Truth About **Worship**	0-7644-0867-4

Exciting Resources for Your Youth Ministry

All-Star Games From All-Star Youth Leaders

The ultimate game book—from the biggest names in youth ministry! All-time no-fail favorites from Wayne Rice, Les Christie, Rich Mullins, Tiger McLuen, Darrell Pearson, Dave Stone, Bart Campolo, Steve Fitzhugh, and 21 others! You get all the games you'll need for any situation. Plus, you get practical advice about how to design your own games and tricks for turning a *good* game into a *great* game!

ISBN 0-7644-2020-8

Last Impressions: Unforgettable Closings for Youth Meetings

Make the closing moments of your youth programs powerful and memorable with this collection of Group's best-ever low-prep (or no-prep!) youth meeting closings. You get over 170 favorite closings, each tied to a thought-provoking Bible passage. Great for anyone who works with teenagers!

ISBN 1-55945-629-9

The Youth Worker's Encyclopedia of Bible-Teaching Ideas

Here are the most comprehensive idea-books available for youth workers. With more than 365 creative ideas in each of these 400-page encyclopedias, there's at least one idea for every book of the Bible. You'll find ideas for retreats and overnighters...learning games... adventures...special projects...affirmations...parties...prayers...music... devotions...skits...and more!

Old Testament   ISBN 1-55945-184-X
New Testament   ISBN 1-55945-183-1

PointMaker™ Devotions for Youth Ministry

These 45 PointMakers™ help your teenagers discover, understand, and apply biblical principles. Use PointMakers as brief meetings on specific topics or slide them into any youth curriculum to make a lasting impression. Includes handy Scripture and topical indexes that make it quick and easy to select the perfect PointMaker for any lesson you want to teach!

ISBN 0-7644-2003-8

More Resources for Your Youth Ministry

Group's Best Discussion Launchers for Youth Ministry

Here's the definitive collection of Group's best-ever discussion launchers! You'll get hundreds of thought-provoking questions kids can't resist discussing...compelling quotes that demand a response... and quick activities that pull kids into an experience they can't wait to talk about. Add zing to your youth meetings...revive meetings that are drifting off-track...and comfortably approach sensitive topics like AIDS, war, cults, gangs, suicide, dating, parents, self-image, and more!

ISBN 0-7644-2023-2

You-Choose-the-Ending Skits for Youth Ministry

Stephen Parolini

Try these 19 hot-topic skits guaranteed to keep your kids on the edge of their seats—because each skit has 3 possible endings! You can choose the ending...flip a coin...or let your teenagers vote. No matter which ending you pick, you'll get a great discussion going about a topic kids care about! Included: no-fail discussion questions!

ISBN 1-55945-627-2

No Supplies Required Crowdbreakers & Games

Dan McGill

This is the perfect book for youth workers on a tight budget. The only supplies you'll need for these quick activities are kids! All 95 ideas are fun, easy-to-do, creative, and tested for guaranteed success!

ISBN 1-55945-700-7

Youth Worker's Idea Depot™

Practical, proven ideas gathered from front-line professionals make this CD-ROM a gold mine of ministry solutions! You can search these ideas instantly—by Scripture...topic...key words...or by personal notes you've entered into your database. You'll get a complete library of ideas—plus a trial subscription to Group Magazine, where you'll discover dozens of new ideas in every issue! For Windows 3.1 or Windows 95.

ISBN 0-7644-2034-8